# Praise for Rick Miller and Be Chief

"It's one thing for a leader such as the Dalai Lama to remind us that human being is every bit as important to life success as is human *doing*, but it's another when a successful business leader nails it too: the *being*, not just the doing of *BE CHIEF* has a pervasive if not oceanic effect on success throughout any enterprise. Not since Peter Drucker declared that our most important managerial assignment is the *management-of-self* do we have a volume that gives us a roadmap to elevate the positive power of anyone's sheer presence. Being Chief is a choice, not a title, says Rick Miller—and it pervades everything a leader does from living your values to creating workplaces of "viral engagement." This is a great teaching tool."

> —David L. Cooperrider, Director, Fowler Center for Business as an Agent of World Benefit and co-Creator of Appreciative Inquiry, Weatherhead School, Case Western Reserve University

"An easy to follow guide that can help leaders at any level unlock the potential in their teams."

> —Tony Hsieh, CEO of Zappos.com Inc., and *New York Times* bestselling author of *Delivering Happiness*

"A must read for anyone looking for an impactful briefing on a lifetime of leadership lessons."

> —Marshall Goldsmith, Thinkers50 #5 world thought leader in leadership

"Reading Rick Miller's unconventional insights and advice on leadership and how to create a winning culture in today's hyper-connected, hyper-competitive world is like having one head slapping ah-ha moment after another. More than a business book, *BE CHIEF* is a valuable reference and resource guide that you will find yourself turning to time and again."

> —Jim McCann, Founder and CEO of 1-800-FLOWERS.COM

"*BE CHIEF* offers a simple and compelling roadmap of options for each of us to unlock our potential while being our authentic selves. As women, we have traditionally been more likely to help others succeed to be Chief rather than focus on ourselves. This special book offers valuable examples of women who do both!"

> —Betsy Myers, Founding Director of the Center for Women & Business at Bentley University, former Director of the White House Office for Women's Outreach, author of *Take The Lead*

"This book reminds us that wherever you sit, it's possible to stand up and lead."

> —Adam Grant, Wharton professor and *New York Times* bestselling author of *Originals, Give and Take* and *Option B*

"By redefining what it means to be a Chief, Rick Miller explains what it takes to truly be successful at work—and in life. Rick makes 'power' a good word again, and teaches us how to have and use it to bring out the best in ourselves and in others."

> —Susan Cain, Co-founder of Quiet Revolution, and *New York Times* bestselling author of *QUIET: The Power of Introverts in A World That Can't Stop Talking*

"Read this one carefully—it is book to think about, not finish. Rick has an inimitable way of getting truth across."

> —Srikumar Rao, author of *Happiness at Work* and creator of Creativity and Personal Mastery

"Rick Miller is one of the most brilliant business thinkers and leaders of today."

> —TEDxWallStreet

"For the new manager or the veteran leader, Rick provides thoughtful insights and true stories about rebooting your approach to the challenge right in front of you."

> —Gail McGovern, President and CEO, American Red Cross

"The leadership values and skills of a chief need not be confined to the C-suite. Rick Miller's outstanding new book, *BE CHIEF*, is a guide to ways in which you can bring your leadership skills up to the highest level, and inspire those around you to do the same. Don't wait for someone to hand you the title, be Chief now!"

> —Daniel H. Pink, *New York Times* bestselling author of *Drive* and *To Sell Is Human*

"Universal truths combined with practical tips and advice based on first-hand experience over decades of driving successful turnarounds. Read this book!"

> —Jack Canfield, co-creator, *Chicken Soup for the Soul* Book Series and *The Success Principles, How to Get From Where You Are to Where You Want to Be*

"Rick Miller has written an engaging text that feels more like a conversation with a friend who wants us to succeed. This book is not about techniques, but of character, and the difference it makes to effective leadership."

—John Hamre, President and CEO, Center for Strategic and International Studies

"Experience-tested guide for bringing back pride, discipline, creativity, and values to your organization and added meaning to your life."

—James Heskett, Baker Foundation Professor Emeritus, Harvard Business School, author of *The Culture Cycle*

"I love Rick Miller's new book, *Be Chief*. Being Chief is what I would call an inside-out process. It's an inner feeling of power—but it's not about control. It's about being confident in your own strengths and in the ability to engage and thrive in your environment. It's attainable whether or not you are in charge—and it's transferable to everyone around you. With personal revelations, case studies, and an easy writing style, Rick shows readers how to be Chief right where they are in any organization."

—Ken Blanchard, coauthor of *The New One Minute Manager*® and *Servant Leadership in Action*

# BE CHIEF

It's A Choice, Not A Title

RICK MILLER

BE CHIEF

Design, graphics and photography
© michael black I BLACK SUN
www.michaelblack.com

*"See simplicity in the complicated.*
*Seek greatness in the small things."*

*Lau Tzu*

*To Diane for teaching me the truth,*
*and to Jack and Casey for teaching me how to laugh.*

# Table of Contents

**Acknowledgements**                                    13

**Introduction**                                        15
   Chiefs in Iraq                                       21

**ONE: Be Chief**                                       27
   Build a Compass                                      28
   Values and Fish Sticks                               31
   Insight and Stairs                                   36
   Creativity and Donuts                                43
   Discipline and Hobbies                               50
   Support and Books                                    56
   A Powerful Chief                                     62
   Choices that Enable Viral Engagement                 65

**TWO: Empower a Team of Chiefs**                       71
   Inspiring Employee Performance                       72
      First Steps                                       74
      Celine, Tom, and Creativity                       90
   Taking On Friendly Fire in a Multinational           97
      Robin, Mike, and Insight                         105
      Changes and Vulnerability                        111

## TWO: Empower a Team of Chiefs [continued]

| | |
|---|---|
| Growing in a Startup | 114 |
| Mary Anne, Dana, and Discipline | 119 |
| The Wisdom of Letting Go | 125 |
| Steering Through a Deathwatch | 129 |
| Mary, Jacquie, and Support | 135 |
| Choices When You're Not in Charge | 141 |
| Serving a Team of Warfighters | 145 |
| Phil, Kathy, and Values | 152 |
| Engaging the Quiet Chiefs | 157 |
| Sustainable Growth | 161 |

## THREE: Your Power Compass      167

## Summary      175

## Index      179

## Bio      182

# Acknowledgements

My journey toward being Chief has been blessed with many great mentors and coaches. In addition to Diane, Jack, and Casey to whom I've dedicated this book, there are countless people to acknowledge and thank for all the help I have gratefully received along the way.

Not surprisingly, learning about being Chief started at home. My folks were strong role models in persistence. My dad built a reputation as a trusted business and community leader over years of service. In a very different set of circumstances, my mother fought decades of serious health challenges that easily could have beaten a lesser woman. She was a fighter. Thank you, Mom and Dad, for the many lessons you taught me and thanks to my two brothers, Ted and Jeff, for the lessons you continue to teach me. I love you all.

I would also like to thank the friends, teachers, and coaches who taught me so much during my time in the Marlboro, Massachusetts public school system and at Bentley University and Columbia University.

Thanks to the many mentors, coworkers, partners, and customers I met during my time at Sperry, Unisys, AT&T, Opus, Lucent, and Being Chief. Thanks also to the many nonprofit leaders and young people I met through The Balance & Stretch Center.

Thanks in particular to Mary Anne Walk, Frank D'Amelio, John Drew, Pat Russo, Dom D'Alessio, Jeff Weitzen, Susan Berg, Vince Molinaro, Maithreyee Dube, Gail McGovern, Steve Schumer, Dorothy Abbott, Mary Slaughter, Pam Hanley Hunter, Paul Madden, Phil Anderson, Alex Mandl, Kristin Haggar, Sue

Jenks, Erin Saxton, Mitch Russo, Seta Shahanian, and Glenn Sanford. I am grateful for your support.

In addition, I acknowledge the positive influence of some of our great academics, authors, and researchers whose work I have enjoyed over many years. These include Thomas Moore, Deepak Chopra, James Kouzes, Eckhardt Tolle, Spencer Johnson, Barry Posner, Peter Drucker, Jack Canfield, Ken Blanchard, Peter Senge, Daniel Kahneman, Thomas Keating, Neale Donald Walsh, Jack Kornfield, John Kotter, Jim Heskett, Norman Vincent Peale, Robert Greenleaf, Stefan Swanepoel, Adam Grant, Daniel Pink, Susan Cain, Malcom Gladwell, Srikumat Rao, Marshall Goldsmith, and Brene Brown.

I acknowledge the thoughtful input of Margaret McBride and Spencer Johnson as well as editing provided by Ann McIndoo, Nils Parker, and Ann Maynard. I also gratefully acknowledge the significant contributions of Jamey Jones whose partnership on this project spans years. I am grateful to Michael Black whose gift of creativity can be seen throughout this book and without whose inspiration this book would not exist. I am also grateful to Justin Sachs and the team at Motivational Press for helping us bring this important message to the world.

# Introduction

Conventional wisdom about Chiefs is all wrong. It says Chiefs are special. Chiefs are chosen. Chiefs have titles. And only those at the top have the power to truly be Chief. Fresh out of business school, I aspired to be among those at the top. I would work hard to move up the ladder in the hope that I could eventually earn a job as a Chief Executive Officer.

For years, I trusted that wisdom. It guided me into and through bigger and bigger roles where I was responsible for generating results for companies in many difficult situations, developing plans for success that focused on a clear vision and a winning strategy to meet customer needs. Those plans often required raising capital, controlling costs, beating competition, and building positive community relationships in order to succeed.

But as I worked my way up through these assignments and had the privilege of working with many individuals who possessed a power that had nothing to do with their title or position, my views shifted. In addition to these traditional areas of focus, I realized that the real key to *sustaining* success is to build an organization where a very high percentage of group members are fully engaged and feel the power of being Chief.

I'll distinguish my use of the word *power* from its usual interpretation where power is equated to position, title, control, or authority. The power of being Chief is not at all conventional. It's a power that comes from within rather than being imposed upon from outside or above. It's a steady, sustainable power rather than a huge burst that fizzles out before long. It's a quiet, insightful power that we tap into to guide our decisions, choices, and future rather than an outside influence that veers us off our course. It's a power that will feel right rather than a power that you question. It's a power that fully engages you and everyone around you.

As any management executive can attest, unleashing that kind of power is easier said than done. Today, reports indicate that seven in 10 workers are not giving 100 percent on the job. Many feel apathetic and powerless. Researchers estimate the cost of this lost productivity at almost $500 billion annually. As an individual, you may be surrounded by disengaged team members, and you may even face that same challenge yourself. By understanding the simple choices outlined in this book, you can solve both problems.

I have also learned that being Chief is actually contagious. And the goal is to create what I call *viral engagement* where everyone feels the opportunity to be Chief, and Chiefs cascade throughout your organization.

In more than 30 years of personal experience I have seen that a single individual's choice to be Chief increases the chances that everyone in the group will engage fully as Chief. Your choices will help those who surround you make their own choices each day that create a positive, change-adaptive culture. You will help every individual lead in their own ways, consistent with their values, their compass, and who they are as individuals. With firm values, stronger relationships will be built inside your group, as well as between groups, that will unlock potential and contribute to sustainable success. The results are amazing. Enabling others to be Chief is the key to building a powerful organization.

The core of an organization's power is solely found in its

people. Their ability, influence, energy, and impact are what drive any organization. I know this because building powerful organizations is what I do. Now, to be clear, I'm not discounting the value of effective, integrated strategies in essential areas like customer relations, competition, financial capital, cost control, community affairs, and climate support. But, though they may be critical to establishing a powerful organization, successful strategies in each of these areas simply create the *conditions* for true power. People, at all tiers and within all departments, are where you'll find the proverbial magic. True Chiefs know how to tap into that power and send it rippling throughout the organization.

Finally, just as being Chief is not about the title, it's also not only about business. People can be Chief in families, communities, governments, social agencies, educational institutions, and ministries. In all cases, I have learned that being Chief means looking inside yourself for answers and direction rather than to others, including so-called experts. The power to be Chief is never given to you by someone else— being Chief is a choice you make. The power is all yours. Being Chief also means relying on a common set of values in both your personal and professional life. Being Chief means you can't do things halfway. You give 100 percent. You own it.

## *Being Chief increases the chances that everyone else will be Chief.*

In this book I share the choices available to any member of a group or organization to increase their power, boost positive capacity, and increase the probability of sustainable growth and success.

The book is divided into three sections:

Part One covers some of my early lessons, successes, and failures, and describes a tool I developed to help people increase their real power. My Power Compass can be used to encourage and enable everyone to increase their clarity, energy, impact, influence, and confidence. These are the true attributes of power that a real Chief wields in an organization.

But since you have your own unique style of leadership, Part One is structured to help you build your own approach to being Chief. At the end of each section, you will be given questions to see how you can translate these new ideas and incorporate them into your own experiences.

Part Two offers five mini case studies describing difficult business situations where teams of Chiefs accomplished amazing turnarounds using the four *directions* of their own Power Compass, fueled by a set of core values unique to the individuals, teams, or organizations. In each case, powerful Chiefs at all levels delivered amazing productivity and remarkable results in very challenging environments. And those around them took notice and responded in kind.

These case studies offer a variety of business situations, including startup, mid-size, and multinational companies, with consumer, corporate, and government customers. They also include stories about a diverse group of women and men who held different levels of authority in departments ranging from finance, sales, and human resources to training and marketing. Each organization worked to solve problems, build powerful teams, and create sustainable growth. The key to success in each case was the ability of Chiefs at all levels to enable the power in themselves and others.

Each business situation, including the one you may be in today, is unique. I offer these diverse stories so that you can learn how you might apply the Power Compass to be Chief in your own unique setting. At the end of each case study, questions are provided to help you determine how the points offered might help you in your own workplace.

Part Three offers you the opportunity to build your own Power Compass. You'll be asked to look at your choices in five areas: discipline, creativity, support, insight, and values, as well as to think about what you stand for. Your "baseline" choices will be translated into a numeric score. Finally, you'll be asked the key question—are you as powerful as you'd like to be? Your Power Compass will help you chart your path. But the journey starts with understanding one crucial fact:

> *The power to be Chief is a choice.*
> *It doesn't come from a title—*
> *it's a choice anyone can make.*

When I started my career, I consistently found myself in difficult business situations. At first, I thought it was bad luck, but over time I realized it was a gift. I learned I was built for turnaround leadership, and I found myself willingly taking roles that others shied away from. Over the first 25+ years of my professional life, I was recruited to lead turnarounds in organizations ranging from a startup to several multinationals. I was given titles including CEO, COO, President, Senior Vice-

President, and Vice-President and General Manager. Utilizing the underlying framework in my Power Compass, I earned a reputation as a turnaround specialist, a fixer, and a sustainable growth expert. One writer even called me a magician. But I can assure you that none of my titles helped our teams succeed, and there was no magic.

I learned to develop a model that became the foundation for everything I did throughout my career. I didn't tout it at the time, but the Power Compass was at work, guiding my actions, decisions, and thoughts as I worked through a diverse career.

Ten years ago, I founded my own company to share my expertise and serve as a confidant to many Chiefs, people with and without the title, in a wide range of companies including several of the most well-known companies on the planet. None of these individuals hired me because of the titles I held. In fact, these leaders are far more likely to refer to me as a student-teacher, a servant leader, and a go-to Chief. I much prefer those labels! Each Chief believed we could work together to drive sustainable growth in their organization, which we did and continue to do by applying the Power Compass. But since those relationships are confidential, you won't see them in this book.

What you will find throughout the book are the most impactful business lessons I've learned to apply with the organizations I served. These lessons have come from a diverse group of wonderful individuals. The teams of powerful people that I had the privilege to work with are those who deserve the credit for whatever success was attributed to me. This book is about their success, which I'm excited to share with you.

Before we dive in, I'll share a story with high stakes and a team of Chiefs that may have saved my life.

## Chiefs in Iraq

Walking off the jet way at Baghdad International Airport, the first thing I noticed was a Rambo-like soldier and his security detail, armed to the teeth—guns, Kevlar bullet-proof jackets, the works. Within seconds, someone jammed a helmet on my head and someone else wrapped me in a bulletproof jacket. Walking rapidly and surrounded by a protective ring of armed guards, I was led through the airport terminal to our transportation: three custom, armor-plated Toyota vehicles cleverly disguised to blend in with the rest of the cars on the streets. This was not your average business trip.

It was February of 2005, and I was making my first trip to Baghdad and the Green Zone, the center of international presence inside Iraq. As President of the Government Solutions Unit at Lucent Technologies, a former U.S. telecommunications company, I had deployed members of my team of specialists to Baghdad months earlier. Our team's first assignment was to build a base of operations inside one of Saddam Hussein's former mansions. But our mission was to implement a citywide wireless communication network to increase public safety in Iraq's capital, something that had never been done before.

The team had been successful with their first big test. Just one month earlier, Iraqi citizens had voted in free elections for the first time in their history. It was a victory for everyone involved and our team took pride in the role we played. Though public safety officials in Baghdad initially displayed skepticism for the new tools at their disposal, by the end of election night those same officials were using our system to identify safe areas before calling family members to tell them where to vote.

They were believers. Many citizens voted safely that night and proudly displayed purple fingers—the mark given to voters that came to symbolize the promise of democracy. But the job was just getting started.

We needed to expand the wireless network beyond Baghdad to the rest of Iraq to support future elections. My role was to engage in meetings with senior Iraqi and U.S. officials to review the project and build on the positive results that had already been established.

My security detail was made up of former British Special Forces members led by Squad Leader Carter, the most intimidating individual I had ever seen. He was 6'2" and 220 pounds with a shaved head, square jaw, eyes that saw right through me, and a gun on each hip. Carter and his team of ten highly trained specialists had only one job that day: to keep me safe. My heart pounded in my chest and my thoughts raced in every direction as we hurried past the other travelers in the airport and made our way toward our vehicles on the terminal's lower level.

Carter took a seat next to me as we tucked into the safety of the bulletproof vehicle. The car doors closed quickly behind us with a quick pop, followed by a brief, pregnant quiet. "Four gunmen will be in the lead car," Carter began, with a point to the car ahead of us. "Another four will be following closely behind us." We were heading toward Baghdad's infamous Airport Road—the one and only way to the Green Zone. Two other gunmen would be with Carter and me in the middle vehicle to complete the convoy.

After ten minutes of roll drills simulating what would happen if we were attacked from different angles during our trip—I would have to move quickly to either the front or back car—we headed for the Green Zone. I wrapped a bandana around my helmet-covered head in case someone caught a glimpse of me through the tinted car windows, and reviewed the emergency escape procedures I had just learned.

As we passed through multiple checkpoints, it was clear the military was on high alert. Recent days had seen an increase in IED (improvised explosive device) activity on Airport Road, evidenced by the constant stream of damaged vehicles along our route. I remember listening to radio conversations between Carter and members of the U.S. Military personnel who were monitoring movements of a "person of interest" as we sped by remnants of broken down military vehicles on both sides of the road. That's when it struck me, *"The person of interest is me."* I was no longer thinking about the plane ride or my upcoming meetings. I focused on my task at hand, making every effort to keep my emotions in check.

Thanks to the efforts of Carter and his team, I was safely ensconced less than an hour later at our facility in the Green Zone, which served as headquarters and our base of operations. Carter and several members of his team would stay with me during my trip. In everything we did while we were at camp, from pre-travel planning and post-travel evaluation reviews to their constant vigilance, these men set a tone of assured focus. Each of us had a job to do. And each of us could trust the other to do his job well. I was grateful to them for enabling me to safely contribute to this next phase of the operation.

Carter and the security team were actually an extension of a larger team assigned to our project in Baghdad. Together, the individuals in this group of dedicated U.S. and Iraqi Military personnel, Lucent employees, and a network of contractors each risked their lives on a daily basis to accomplish the mission. My job was to support this high-performing team and get them what they needed to continue to build on their initial success.

Overall, my meetings with senior members of the U.S. and Iraqi Military, as well as senior Iraqi government officials, went well. The critical nature of our assignment was acknowledged and added resources were assigned to support the mission. In one particularly important session, I met with the Iraqi Minister of the Interior along with Ed Eldridge, our project manager and another Chief, to offer an update on our project.

## *An entire team can step up to be Chief. When they do, the results are magnified.*

It was months before the next phase of implementation was completed. When we finished, the expanded communication network again played a vital role ensuring the safety of citizens who voted in October on a Constitutional Referendum and again in December to select the Iraqi Council of Representatives, this time with full Sunni participation and a 76 percent voter turnout. In the most challenging environment many of us had ever worked in, our team demonstrated productivity and resilience, working long hours while bombs periodically burst around us.

Who was the Chief in this mission? If you go by conventional definition and looked at an organizational chart, I was Chief. But I don't define Chief the way most people do.

When I first arrived at Baghdad airport, Squad Leader Carter was Chief, to be sure, but so was every individual who risked his or her life to get me safely to the Green Zone. More broadly, the high-risk nature of this assignment mandated that every member of our team operated as Chief in his or her areas of responsibility.

It is a credit to every Chief on our team that we accomplished our mission.

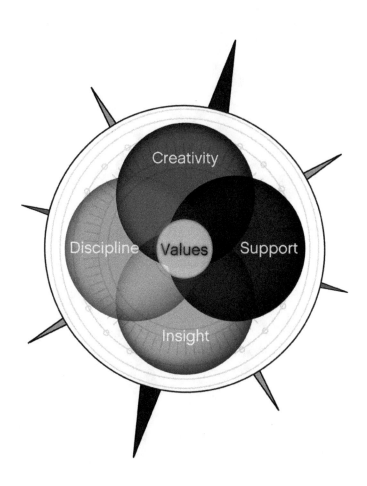

# ONE

# Be Chief

*I have been fortunate to be mentored by many kind people. Their generosity and wisdom enabled me to develop an approach to unlocking the power inside myself as well as the potential of those around me. What follows is a description of that approach, and a simple tool—a "Compass"—that anyone can use to help them find their way to unlocking their own power and the power in those around them. In this section you'll learn to do just that.*

## Build a Compass

There are lots of ideas about leadership and where it should come from. I believe leadership, in general, and being Chief, in particular, is a choice available to everyone. To illuminate this choice—this set of choices, really—I developed the Power Compass.

Growing up, we didn't travel much. My dad worked hard and so when it was time for vacation, the last thing he wanted to do was pile us into the family car for a long drive to a new sight or city. He just wanted to take it easy and relax. Rather than taking extravagant vacations, which we couldn't afford, we took small day trips or simply drove to a familiar place using a different route. My favorite destination was a farm 20 miles from home that served the best ice cream on the planet. Maybe ice cream led to my love of roadmaps and my understanding of the importance of a compass: there's usually something good waiting for you when you get where you want to go.

Consider roadmaps. Your driving preferences may change during different times and under different circumstances, but a roadmap will always offer alternatives. At times the most direct way from A to B may not be the best way for you. Sometimes you want to go fast. Other times you want to slow down and enjoy the ride. Or, you might want to take a detour and travel through certain communities to reach your destination. And sometimes you may just want to take a new road. Then tomorrow, when both your starting point and destination change, a roadmap will continue to serve you well.

Early in my career I relied on what I learned about roadmaps as an analogy for life. I believed that no matter where I wanted to go there would always be a road to get me there. But the analogy let me down when I found myself wanting to go places where others hadn't ventured before—where there was no paved road. It was then that I came to appreciate the value of a compass.

I learned that a compass is the ideal tool when you know what direction you'd like to go, but you are faced with the task of blazing a new trail. You might get advice and counsel from others that sets you off in the right direction, but getting to a new place will require your ability to listen closely to your own intuition, guided by your values, and to do things your own way. You will find that you make stronger choices and are more successful as you get better at connecting what you *do* to who you *are*. It is from here that your true power derives. That's your Power Compass.

As you will see throughout these pages, the Power Compass will help guide you through the choices you'll have to make as you carve out your path, ensuring that *what you do* stays aligned and consistent with *who you are*—thereby ensuring that your decisions are powerful.

Each of the Power Compass's five elements—Values, Insight, Creativity, Discipline, Support—offers choices that can be made by anyone, independent of level or position in any group or organization, to build success by creating a culture where people excel.

Enabling a team of Chiefs starts with you and your ability to answer important questions, such as:

- How can living my *values* bring out the best in me and those around me?
- How can I develop *insight* to learn more about myself?
- How can I use *creativity* to increase my positive impact?
- How can I use *discipline* to manage better?
- How can I *support* others to increase their positive impact?

Your Power Compass will help you answer those questions and determine the areas where you can increase your power, which we will discuss in Part Three of this book. The Power Compass has been extensively road tested and will help you, your team, and your organization navigate a path to success—yes, even in tough times.

By tapping into the power you already hold, you have the ability to be Chief whenever you choose to step into the role. And the values, history, and perspectives that make you who you are (and will determine the Chief you become) are an excellent place to begin.

## Values and Fish Sticks

You expect to learn a lot when you go to college. I know I did when I enrolled as an undergrad at Bentley College.

While I have lots of great memories from school, one specific class and teacher stand out. In the fall semester of my junior year, I took a marketing class taught by a part-time faculty member who had been very successful in the business world. When he walked into class on day one, Mr. Malcolm Harris began the course with words that would change my life. He said:

> Good morning ladies and gentlemen. Welcome to Marketing 101. I am here to teach you the two most important lessons required for anyone to have a real shot at achieving big-deal status in business. The truth of the matter is that there are really only two keys to business: First, you must understand customers; and second, you must understand competition. I may be the only teacher to tell you this: The best job to teach you about customers and competition is a job in sales. Get your degree and go get a sales job. Take the risk and go on commission.

I nearly dropped my pencil. A job in sales? Like most college juniors, I was convinced I could do anything, but Mr. Harris had thrown down a gauntlet that rocked me out of my comfort zone. The idea of taking a job in sales caused me to panic. And I could swear I smelled fish sticks.

I grew up in a middle-class family where money was often tight. My parents attempted to shield my brothers and me from the family financial issues, but as the oldest of three, I had a sense of when money was running low. My biggest clue came from what was on the dinner table: fish sticks.

When we were served cheap, breaded fish sticks on consecutive nights, I knew that money was tight. I grew up associating fish sticks with things not going well. I hated the taste of them and the bad feelings I had when I ate them. Now, fish sticks were the unlikely embodiment of my fear of failure, of my anxiety over financial instability. In fact, one of the reasons I was sitting in Harris' class, the reason I was pursuing business, was the opportunity to earn a good living. I wanted to be successful, earn a stable income, and make sure that I would never have to eat fish sticks again.

Now I had a professor I trusted telling me "the truth" that if I wanted to be a big deal in business, I needed to take a job with variable earnings that could potentially put frozen, breaded fish back on my dinner plate if I didn't make the sale.

*Facing your fear and learning to live your values are an essential part of being Chief and building a team of Chiefs.*

I could feel fear in the pit of my stomach, announcing itself in a way that always seems to come when you have unwittingly put yourself in a defining moment. I could walk out of the class and pursue something else or I could stay and do what it took to succeed in the field I wanted. Although fearful, I pushed ahead, trusting my teacher's advice. Three years later I finished my instruction as a computer sales trainee. By deciding to go into sales I had taken the first step toward increasing my power. I was bringing all of who I was into what I was going to do—even my fears and my pain points.

Choosing to face the truth and confront my fear was an early lesson that prepared me for what it would take to be Chief. Fish sticks were a motivating force (so help me, I was not going to eat fish sticks again) that eventually came to embody a value instead of a fear. I chose to bring who I was—my history, my perspective, my value system—into the work I was doing and, as I rose through the ranks, I realized that it was something that people around me responded to. By living my personal values in the professional sphere, I was able to lead in a way that was demonstrative instead of discursive; I gained authority through my character and my actions instead of my title or my demands. It also helped those around me to be Chief. Values are the foundation of relationships and of being Chief. And although my dad was my early role model, I have been blessed with many other mentors who reinforced this central message. Great relationships grow with compassion, forgiveness, respect, and empathy.

I also agree with the wisdom offered in the Talmud, the central text of mainstream Judaism that offers: *the highest form of wisdom is kindness.* We all have our own unique journey and a choice of which values we embrace. I have chosen four as the basis for my relationships: truth, service, connection, and equality.

I believe truth is found in listening, learning, and feeling; and that the inner peace derived from truth brings wisdom and understanding.

I believe it is our responsibility to serve others in need with empathy and that we must learn to be humble as we administer aid and be open to receiving from those being aided.

I believe we are all connected in ways we have yet to fully understand.

I believe that we are all equal, and that every individual has an ability to teach and to learn.

But values are very personal and while I believe deeply in my values, you should have your own list. Your values are the foundation of your power to be Chief. It's important to take the time to determine what you stand for, but your power comes when you choose to regularly take a stand and act consistently in alignment with those values. As mine have done for me, your values will form a strong foundation as you set your own goals. They will also be critical to your ability to enable others to be Chief.

**Your Turn.** Please take some time to reflect on your own values. How can living your *values* bring out your best and the best in those around you? Consider the following questions:

- Have I spent the time to determine what values I want to stand for?
- What are those values?
- How can I make my values visible to others in how I speak, write, and act?

e

## Insight and Stairs

By the time I arrived at the local sales office of Sperry Univac, the original computer manufacturing company in Wellesley, Massachusetts, I was a 21-years old college graduate who was ready to start my career.

The problem was I did not yet have a job. After Mr. Harris' class and graduation, I knew I wanted a sales job in the fast-growing computer industry. I had interviewed with some of the big corporate leaders like IBM, Digital Equipment Corporation, Data General, Honeywell, and Prime Computer. But I had no job offers.

Now I was standing in front of the receptionist at Sperry, résumé in hand. "I'd like to speak to the branch manager, please."

She looked taken aback and slowly reached for the paper I was holding out to her. "Do you have an appointment?"

"No. No I don't. But I don't need more than a few minutes."

She peered at me over the top of her glasses and pursed her lips. "I'm afraid our branch manager isn't available. I'll be happy to give this to him," she said, setting my résumé to her right, "but I don't believe we're hiring."

I wasn't surprised by what she said. I knew it was a long shot to walk in unannounced and unexpected. I turned around and started walking toward the door, but as I did a strong feeling came over me: *I should wait.* I didn't know it at the time, but the insight that came from being able to listen to that gut feeling gave me the power that would help me become Chief. I turned back around.

"What time do you think he'll be available?"

The receptionist assured me that she had no idea if the branch manager would be available anytime in the near future, if at all. She also shared that, again, to the best of her knowledge, the company was not hiring. I let her know that I was perfectly willing to wait. I took a seat in the waiting room, looking at the spiral staircase in front of me that no doubt led to where I wanted to be, and thought about the strong feeling in my gut and what I would say to the branch manager when I met him.

An hour later, another woman walked by. She stopped in her path and, with a glance in my direction, started murmuring something to the receptionist. "*Is she asking about me?*" I wondered. The receptionist confirmed it:

"He wants to see Mr. Laferriere." Her voice dropped, "Another applicant. No appointment. I told him that Mr. Laferriere would not see him without an appointment."

The woman glanced my way again and slid my résumé on to the stack of folders she was carrying. An hour later, the receptionist's phone rang.

"Hi Judi," the receptionist's eyes then darted in my direction, "Yes, of course." I perked up as she hung up the phone. "Mr. Laferriere can see you now," she said. "His office is just up those spiral stairs, first door to the left." I was excited and glad that I had waited as I walked up the circular staircase to his office.

My future boss' deep voice resonated through the room before I even had a chance to close the door: "So I understand you're looking for a job."

When I met Dick, I had no idea that he would become one of the most influential people in my life. What I remember most about meeting him was our great conversation about school, sports, and family. It was clear that Dick had a strong set of values, and that he cared deeply about people. I knew I could learn a lot from him. Then we got down to brass tacks.

"These," Dick said as he pointed to a large stack of papers on his desk, "are résumés I've received over the past several months. They're all from recent college graduates like you, and they're all vying for a spot in our computer sales training program."

It was a big stack, presumably filled with applications from people as qualified as I was for the role (or more so). He said that he did not have time to look through all the résumés, let alone to schedule and conduct multiple interviews to select the best candidate.

"But you are hiring?" I finally mustered.

"We weren't," he replied, "Until yesterday. I got a call from my boss giving me the approval to hire a new sales trainee. We haven't even announced it yet."

I thought about the woman who had pulled my résumé from the receptionist's desk. Judi. She was the only other person in the office who knew about the call.

## *Learn to truly listen to the voice inside you and to trust your insight.*

I started my first job as a sales trainee at Sperry the following Monday. At that time, Sperry was using the tagline, "We understand how important it is to listen." It was a coincidence that was not lost on me. Listening to my inner voice—to my gut—helped me land my first job. In the next fifteen years at Sperry, I had many opportunities to listen to coworkers, customers, partners, and many others, and I learned how much effort is required when you truly listen. That investment paid big returns.

Years after I benefited from listening to my own voice at Sperry, I was fortunate to get a powerful reminder about insight from a six-year-old girl who I will call Melissa. I met Melissa when I was volunteering at the Morristown Rehabilitation Hospital. I spent a summer working with the rehab staff in a 100 degree heated pool where we would stretch the muscles of kids with various physical challenges. Among many great kids, Melissa stood out. While her body was bent and curled in unnatural ways, her smile was constant, and the joy she displayed when in the water was felt by everyone around her.

Melissa reminded me to be present and to enjoy each moment. She showed me how to be still with the patience she displayed as she waited in a wheelchair for her turn in the pool, taking in all that was going on around her. As she interacted with other kids, her kind manner taught me to be accepting. I never saw Melissa show frustration or heard her raise her voice. Melissa showed me how to be grateful every time she said thank you. She also showed me how to be generous as she gave of herself more than anyone I have ever met.

It is said that when the student is ready, the teacher will appear. As I practiced what Melissa taught me, I found I learned a lot about myself. I am blessed to have had such a wonderful teacher.

Being Chief requires us to develop insight. It is as much about being as it is about being *Chief*. Insight is a key to increasing your confidence, effectiveness, and, since your power increases as you connect what you do to who you are, deepening your self-understanding through insight will deepen your power. In each of the five business cases outlined in Part Two, I'll share how million and billion dollar organizations facing market crashes or operating in war zones benefited from the lessons I learned from an amazing six-year-old girl. Insight can come from the simplest experiences and from the places you least expect it. Always be on the lookout for gems of insight that can guide your path in life.

There are five ways a leader can learn more about themselves. Specifically, Chiefs choose to be:

- Present
- Still
- Accepting
- Generous
- Grateful

**Be Present:** When you become totally aware and conscious, you can use all of your senses to learn everything possible in the current moment. Specifically, when you give 100 percent of your attention to the people you spend time with, you will find that your relationships become much more fulfilling.

*Insight is the understanding
that comes from self-awareness.*

**Be Still:** Contrary to many Western cultural norms, perhaps our most important choice is to develop the deeper understanding and truth that comes with being still. To maintain inner balance, choose the tranquility and peace of stillness. In that peaceful state, you will develop the ability to trust and have confidence in your own voice.

**Be Accepting:** When you choose to accept people and circumstances for who and what they are, you can escape the frustration of trying to change them. Try to take a nonjudgmental approach to people to open yourself to the potential of clarity and deeper relationships.

When you accept the past and remain receptive to circumstances and people, you can open yourself to the possibilities of learning from all situations and from every individual. When you accept your current reality with a certain degree of detachment, you will find that things come to you with a fraction of the effort otherwise required.

**Be Generous:** When you choose to be charitable with your possessions, your money, and your time, you will experience inner satisfaction despite "having less." When you are kind, helpful, encouraging, and gentle with others, you may even feel aligned with a higher purpose. Try to balance giving with receiving to eliminate much of the possibility of arrogance; this way you can remain genuinely and truly humble.

**Be Grateful:** It is easy to be grateful when things are going well. It takes inner strength and composure to remain grateful when facing life's inevitable difficult periods. The grace required to face tough times and remain thankful is a blessing. Try to remain appreciative of the opportunity to learn lessons from the challenges you face.

Insight is an integral element of being a powerful Chief and enabling a team of Chiefs. A real Chief does not abrasively influence the world around him or her but, rather, considers a wider perspective that begins on the inside. By taking the time and effort to be present, still, accepting, generous, and grateful, the more difficult aspects of being Chief will suddenly take on new meaning. From this vantage point, true growth—both personal and professional—is far more likely.

**Your Turn.** Please take some time to reflect on your own experience with listening to yourself and developing insight. How can you develop *insight* to learn more about yourself and to build a team of Chiefs? Consider the following questions:

- What can I do to stay present and live in the current moment?
- How can I quiet my mind to listen to the voice inside me?
- Do I accept people and circumstances as they are in the moment?
- How can I be more generous with my time and possessions?
- Am I grateful for life's gifts?

## Creativity and Donuts

When I graduated from Sperry's eighteen-month sales trainee program, I was assigned a "pots and pans" sales territory—sales jargon for a group of small accounts with no Sperry presence—where my sales manager could afford for me to make mistakes. Although my formal training was completed, everyone in the office, including me, knew my real education in sales was just beginning.

I was assigned to go after new local government customers in eastern Massachusetts and my objective was to replace their incumbent IBM equipment with Sperry equipment. New business is typically the toughest type of sales assignment because you have so much to do before you can talk about what you are there to sell. It can take weeks and months to establish the personal and company credibility necessary before a potential customer will even consider any meaningful discussion about your products and services.

My youthful appearance and lack of experience, when added to Sperry's shortage of local government reference accounts and the relative strength of IBM, made this a challenging first assignment. To complicate things, my sales manager was involved in a big project and unable to spend much time with me. I was on my own.

I began making cold calls on civic leaders, including the soon-to-be mayor of the City of Lynn, Massachusetts. In sales training, I learned that identifying the power players in any organization isn't necessarily determined by simply looking at the top of an organization chart. In fact, after talking to people at town hall, I learned that it was a woman named Grace, the

Purchasing Director, who truly ran the City of Lynn. Grace was an incredible individual—she was a strong, smart, committed, and enthusiastic public servant whose department operated with the highest level of integrity.

In my first sales visit with Grace, I remember the look she gave her secretary as she instructed her to schedule me for fifteen minutes the next day—"That is, if you're interested in coming back," she joked. The next day, Grace questioned me crisply: "What other cities use your products? How long have your products been in the market? What kinds of savings have other customers seen when they implemented your products?" I must have done something right, because at the end of fifteen minutes, she called her deputy to join us and gave instructions to get more details about our offerings. I was both excited and proud of myself for getting the appointment and determined to make the opportunity count.

Over the next week, I called on her deputy and other members of her staff every day, always arriving early, accompanied with a big box of donuts. By learning who liked which donuts, I also learned the faces and names of every member of her department. I learned how the city functioned and where it was experiencing problems. As I got to know the underpinnings of the city, I learned an important fact: the purchasing department was planning to release a request for proposal (RFP) for an upgrade or replacement of IBM systems. That was my chance.

"Replacing IBM at Lynn is a long shot," my sales manager said with an emphatic shake of his head.

I really thought he'd be more enthusiastic about the idea. "Well, yes, I know that," I continued. "But we've been added to the bidders list. We've got a shot."

"I can't give you a team to chase after this with," he said. "Resources are too tight." That made sense to me. The office was small and I was still unproven when it came to landing major accounts. I was on my own in answering my first bid response. It was all up to me to create success.

The entire RFP process took months. With no other prospects, I was at Lynn City Hall four out of five days each week. I was completely focused on landing the account, sinking the long shot. While I did my best to establish a relationship with Bill, the Data Processing Manager, it was obvious that staying with IBM was his clear preference. I also saw a lot of Grace, but kept my distance from those in her department who were responsible for the IBM replacement RFP process. I knew they needed to ensure objectivity in the process.

I continued to learn all I could about how Lynn operated, where problems existed, and how our products could both increase efficiency and save money. I thought about the sales process seemingly every night.

Finally, it was time to submit our bid. Using all the resources I had, and all the information I had learned by spending so much time at the City Hall, I created and submitted my first written RFP response. Nervous, excited, and questioning myself about what I might have forgotten, I waited for the decision.

My focus, commitment to the project, due diligence, and creativity paid off. When I learned that we had won the bid, I was ecstatic and shaking with excitement. It was worth every minute I had invested in preparing the RFP. Although I was anxious to celebrate, I did not immediately tell anyone at the office. Instead, I invited my sales manager to attend the Lynn City Council meeting where the award was to be made final.

As expected, IBM management attended the meeting and attempted to stop the contract from being awarded to Sperry based on "issues" with the process. They claimed their submission must have been misinterpreted and requested more time for clarification. The City Council members were looking at each other with concern until the Chair recognized Grace to address their issues. In her normal, no-nonsense style, Grace addressed each objection and we won a unanimous vote from the City Council. My sales manager looked over to me, speechless with surprise. I was beaming, feeling both honored and thrilled to have won the bid.

We met with Grace after the meeting. "Congratulations you two," she said, shaking each of our hands.

"Grace—Can I call you Grace?" My manager held his tongue until he received a permission-giving nod and one of Grace's infectious smiles. "Can you share your process with us?"

"You mean, why did you win?" she smiled again. "Well, in addition to being the lowest qualified bidder, your team worked hard and smart throughout the process."

My manager cleared his throat at the mention of the "team" assigned to the bid. Grace continued: "And they demonstrated honesty and kindness that were recognized by my entire staff. These are qualities we look for when we build new relationships."

Reflecting back, Grace's words made an impression that stuck with me. She had summarized my strategy succinctly. Without guidance, I had built a tool to help me succeed as Chief. The tool had four components: Intensity (hard work), Intelligence (smart work), Integrity (honest work) and Kindness. I started to refer to this approach as my i3K strategy. Later, my i3K tool would help me find these qualities within others—recognizing the Chief within them. Teams built on an i3K foundation generally excel.

*Build your own compass and*
*create your future.*

Instead of adhering to the more traditional definition of creativity, which links it to innovation, I propose that creativity is actually the ability to manifest, or create, the future.

Being Chief offers the view that there are five main choices when it comes to creativity. We are at our creative best when we connect our choices. Chiefs create the future when they:

- Feel
- Think
- Speak
- Write
- Act

**Feel:** Perhaps your strongest energy and greatest truth come from your emotions. Feelings provide a great window into your unique and personal truth and are expressed through an accurate personal barometer—your body. When you learn to tune into your body's signals, it won't mislead you. Trust your instincts, intuition, and "gut feelings," and listen to them.

**Think:** Active thinking is the conscious awareness of the creative process. Therefore, try to manage your thoughts. With practice, you can change negative patterns as soon as you become aware of them. You can use optimistic future scenarios, while focusing on the positive nature of what is happening, and take advantage of the powers of visualization to improve performance and build energy.

**Speak:** Spoken words have inspired and incited. Speeches have always been an effective tool to influence people. Relationships can be strengthened or weakened based on the care used with the spoken word. Select your words carefully.

**Write:** Understand the power of the pen as a creative force to influence others. You might choose to believe the energy created by your written word can influence others and impact life. Your written word is no less powerful in its ability to positively influence your own behavior and to create your future.

## Creativity is the ability to bring the future into existence.

**Act:** Your actions offer the most visible form of creation. You can take conscious action that builds on your feelings, thoughts, speech, and writing, and hold yourself accountable for your actions because you understand that action is powerful.

Do you know people who seem to have "tailwinds" that help them move with ease in everything they do? I do! When I act in a way that is synchronized with who I am, I find that things seem to happen more easily for me, too. When synchronized, I experience an increase in my power, and I find that my happiness increases as well.

Chiefs do not manifest the future by barking orders from up above but rather by connecting different forms of internal and external creativity to maintain and convey integrity and to unite an organization of people around its goals. That's how groups create real power. Creating the future is not about waving a magic wand; creativity is a concrete practice that enables, and even catalyzes, a team of Chiefs infused with a purpose.

**Your Turn.** Please take some time to reflect on your own experience with *creativity*. How can you use creativity to increase your positive impact and build a team of Chiefs? Consider the following questions:

- How can I use my gut feelings for guidance?
- What can I do to stop negative thinking when I become aware of it?
- Knowing that words are powerful, how can I be more conscious of my own word choice?
- How can I write to express what I feel and what I think?
- How can I act in ways that are consistent with what I feel, think, and say?

## Discipline and Hobbies

My early jobs in sales and sales management helped me learn how critical discipline is in building strong relationships. My first job was to meet new people, build a positive first impression, and establish my credibility by quickly providing information that could be of value to a prospective customer. I had to convince people that it was worth their while to spend more time with me. When I moved up into sales management, my job was to work with former peers to enable them to be more successful. I had to convince this team of professionals, all older and more experienced than me, that I could help them make a lot more money. In both roles, discipline helped me with the clarity and focus I needed to build trust and communicate effectively.

As a sales representative, I learned to establish credibility and trust early by quickly letting a potential customer know I understood their needs and had a solution that fit. Clarity and focus were key. In each case I developed a plan for every sales call and followed the plan when I could. I planned the work and worked the plan, but I also learned that adjusting quickly to situations as they developed would be every bit as important to my success. I needed to learn to think on my feet.

I also learned that if everything else is equal, people buy from people they like spending time with. I learned to listen and connect with people on topics they cared about outside of work. My goal was to find their hobby. Once we started to swap stories about our respective hobbies, we were far more likely to do business together.

As the saying goes, "Some people don't care how much

you know until they know how much you care." I learned that listening to others and sharing stories about hobbies helped me reach a better level of understanding and likeability with any potential customer because we were sharing what we cared about. Over time, people see you in many situations and come to understand what you are really all about and who you are. While family and friends usually know you best, newer acquaintances will be interested in a deeper relationship if you hold a shared perspective on important topics. What you do and how you do it can teach others about your values. I learned that shared values could be a powerful bridge toward trust.

I also learned that there is a straightforward and powerful way to help a new acquaintance understand your values: simply give them your complete and undivided attention when they are speaking.

When you give someone your undivided attention, you let the person know you are ready to serve his or her needs. They will feel more comfortable with you because they see that you are open to learning from them. At that moment, nothing is more important to you than your conversation.

### *Learning to be disciplined in everything you do will increase your power as Chief.*

When I was promoted to lead a team of what had been my peers as sales manager, discipline was just as critical. The challenge at times seemed daunting. Several members of my sales team were on the same team four years earlier, when I was hired as a sales trainee. Now I was their boss. It helped that I knew them each as individuals and had a sense for each of their styles and views, but the key to our success was to regularly and predictably involve all team members in any decision we could make as a team. We planned the work and worked the plan, together. We set our objectives, built our strategy, and developed a dashboard of leading indicators to measure our progress, as a group. I also worked hard to ensure my one-on-one conversations with team members were effective and that they took responsibility for their success. While I was always 51 percent responsible, communication is a two-way street—it helps to remember that communication is the joint construction of meaning. While what we each said was important, it was more important to know what the other person actually heard.

To create a joint construction of meaning, communication and understanding must travel in both directions. Once again, I learned that being Chief was less about being a better talker and more about being a better listener.

Being Chief involves five main choices when it comes to discipline. Specifically, Chiefs choose to:

- Envision
- Strategize
- Plan Tactics
- Implement and Measure
- Adjust

**Envision:** Everyone wants to be part of something meaningful and important. Many believe that it is the duty of an individual high in the organization to provide a gripping vision for the rest of the organization to follow. Everyone has the opportunity to choose his or her own vision—one that is personally compelling. Being Chief is not about dictating an organization's beliefs; it's about helping to shape them along with each member of the team.

> *Discipline is an orderly pattern of behavior that increases the likelihood of a desired outcome.*

**Strategize:** It is true that those at the top of any organization determine strategy, set goals, and allocate resources to support a vision. Even if you're given a strategy to work with from your boss, you might find that you need to develop your own strategy to accomplish the job. And when you include members of your team to do it, you're more likely to perform better as a unit.

**Plan Tactics:** The quality of detailed tactical planning behind each component of a strategy will directly impact the probability of the strategy's success. Develop your own strategy, and also encourage all members of your team to set their own work goals and make sure their input is heard.

**Implement and Measure:** Success occurs when you plan the work and work the plan. All members of an organization have a role to play and are accountable for the quality they put into their part of implementation. Measuring with granularity maximizes the chance of success at each step of a process, particularly when you can use leading indicators that are predictive of success, rather than lagging indicators that simply measure results.

**Adjust:** Things change. Organizations that succeed are those where everyone in the group consistently looks for opportunities created by change and then exploits them with open lines of communication and quick, disciplined adjustment. This is the ultimate goal of a completely engaged workforce. It's not easy but it's critical to long-term success.

Enabling a team of Chiefs is about creating an environment that encourages every individual to engage in their own form of self-discipline and where everyone can feel powerful. That's not to say discipline never comes from above, but by empowering each member of an organization to be accountable, discipline from above will not be required as frequently.

**Your Turn.** Please take some time to reflect on your own experience with *discipline*. How can you use discipline to manage better and build a team of Chiefs? Consider the following questions:

- How can I describe my work and the work of others in a broad, positive context?
- How can I build specific approaches to accomplish group success with others?
- Do I develop detailed tactical plans to reach shared goals with others? If not, how can I do so?
- Do I execute with detailed plans, track progress with metrics, and hold myself accountable for performance? If not, how can I do so?
- Do I anticipate changes, accept input from all sources and communicate regularly? If not, how can I do so?

## Support and Books

My dad was the earliest influence in my life and the one that shaped the very essence of who I am, how I work, and how I live. My first recollection of my dad's work goes back to when I was seven years old. My dad had started a new job as a personnel administrator for the Heald Machine Company in Worcester, Massachusetts. Heald was one of the few non-union machine tool manufacturers in the Worcester area and Dad's job was to support the work force of 1,700 in all areas of human resources. He spent time working to support employee issues regarding compensation, performance management, benefits, hiring, grievances, safety issues, service awards, and anything else they needed.

Dad saw his job as an opportunity to create a culture of mutual respect and support between labor and management. In his 27 years at Heald, during difficult economic times that saw the work force drop to less than 700 people, there was never a single vote to start a union. In my mind, the reason was simple: workers at Heald didn't need a union to look after them when they had my dad. My dad had built a reputation as a trusted leader during his years of service. He acted as Chief. Independent of his level or title, management trusted him and the workers followed his lead.

I was fortunate to learn from many other strong leaders like my dad in the workforce at Sperry. But my formal education didn't stop when I entered the workforce. Five years into my career at Sperry, I was selected to participate in the Executive MBA Program at Columbia University, where I expanded my solid foundation with an accomplished group of executive classmates and great professors. Among many great lessons, one stands out.

The specific class included the study of Robert Greenleaf's seminal work entitled *Servant Leadership*. The story describes a band of men on a long journey that is sustained by the spirit and song of a servant named Leo. All goes well until Leo disappears and the group falls into disarray. They cannot succeed in their journey without him—Leo, the *servant*.

Greenleaf's message was clear. Leadership is not defined by level in an organization. It is an opportunity for everyone. My dad would have agreed.

My time at Columbia also prompted my appreciation for the wisdom found in many management books.

Over the years I have read lots of pages with lots of words. One of my very favorites is *The One Minute Manager* by Spencer Johnson and Ken Blanchard. The book offers invaluable insight into the challenges of leading people using three simple, powerful principles—goal-setting, recognition, and feedback. I have kept a first edition copy on my desk since 1982, when it was first published.

Another favorite is *The Leadership Challenge: How to Get Extraordinary Things Done in Organizations* by James Kouzes and Barry Posner. It has had a great influence on my thinking about supporting others. But I have probably been most impacted by Jim Heskett and John Kotter's *Corporate Culture and Performance*. These two Harvard Business School researchers provided the first comprehensive critical analysis in 1992 of how the culture of a corporation powerfully influences its economic performance. Heskett and Kotter outlined the components of what they termed a *performance enhancing (PE) culture*.

The authors studied both the actions and attributes of people who had succeeded. They acknowledged the challenges of building a performance-enhancing culture. Notably for me, they also quantified the powerful implications of culture, good and bad, in a small chart summarizing the performance of over 30 companies measured over an 11-year period:

## Costs of Low-Performance Cultures
Eleven Year Growth Comparison

| GROWTH | POSITIVE PE Cultures Average Performance | NEGATIVE PE Cultures Average Performance |
|---|---|---|
| Revenue | 682% | 166% |
| Employment | 282% | 36% |
| Stock Price | 901% | 74% |
| Net Income | 756% | 1% |

The culture of an organization, whether positive or negative, plays a major role in the company's performance. Does your company have a positive or negative performance-enhancing (PE) culture?

Here is research-based proof that focusing on employee engagement and culture is critical to producing sustainable economic performance.

Again I saw support for the lessons my dad taught me and realized that solid footing could come from many sources.

*Being open to input from varied sources can help you support others as you form a solid foundation for being Chief.*

As I have shared, my role model for support was my dad. Watching the way he reacted to different situations, I learned how important it is to model the behavior you expect of others.

He always kept his head when times got tough. With his consistency and values, he also taught me to inspire others.

Listening to dad's work stories taught me that it was management's job to enable the success of workers by ensuring adequate training. Dad also let me know how important it is to encourage others—everyone likes to be recognized. With seemingly endless patience, he also showed me how to learn by questioning. Dad never pretended to have all the answers and always sought to understand the views of others.

Being Chief includes the lessons that my dad shared with me and involves exercising five main choices when it comes to support. Specifically, Chiefs choose to:

- Model
- Inspire
- Enable
- Encourage
- Question

**Model:** Dad did more than simply talk the talk; he was the talk. The credibility required to build trust and earn respect comes with consistency. Try to consistently align what you do to who you are. In addition, there is simply no better way to lose the credibility you need to guide others than to say one thing and do another.

**Inspire:** People are often motivated by others who consistently do the right things, the right way. As with modeling, leaders inspire others to want to follow them because of who they are rather than by simply what they say. Doing things that are visibly consistent with your values is the best way to inspire others.

**Enable:** In service to others, look for opportunities to both help people expand their knowledge and abilities and provide freedom for individuals to exercise new capabilities—in essence, enabling the individuals to choose to be Chiefs themselves. Everyone benefits when people learn new things and feel empowered and accountable.

**Encourage:** Everyone likes to be recognized. All forms of recognition can increase engagement, from simple thank-you's to more elaborate and formal awards for small or large groups. In all cases, as individuals receive encouragement, they are more likely to feel confident and supported as they continue to grow.

**Question:** Cultivate curiosity. To understand the connection between people and ideas, ask a lot of questions. You can also use the technique of questioning to challenge others in their assumptions and to expand their thinking about new opportunities. A central part of questioning is the ability to truly listen to what is being offered to you.

*Active listening requires you to use all of your senses and is another important part of being Chief.*

Enabling a team of Chiefs is more about giving support than receiving it. People feel powerful when they serve others. Service is the highest form of leadership and a key to sustainable growth.

**Your Turn.** Please take some time to reflect on your own experience with creating a solid foundation of *support*. How can you support others to increase their positive impact and build a team of Chiefs? Consider the following questions:

- Do I "walk the talk" to demonstrate what I believe to others?
- How can I motivate others more with who I am, rather than what I say?
- Do I actively support others with what they need once I understand their needs?
- What can I do to cheer for others?
- Do I ask others about their views, motives, and assumptions, and always listen to the responses? If not, what opportunities do I have to do so?

# A Powerful Chief

Values, Support, Creativity, Discipline, and Insight are the foundation of what it means to be Chief. They make up the Power Compass that guides which direction you take at any given moment. Over my 15 years at Sperry/Unisys, I met many amazing people who embodied these key concepts. Regardless of their resumes, experience, or titles, I learned many lessons from these wonderful mentors. Better still, I was often inspired to action by their energy and example. But it was during a 30-minute car ride in Tallahassee that I truly experienced the power of viral engagement. The feeling I had on that short trip remains with me to this day.

It happened shortly after being named as Director of Marketing for Unisys' State Government unit, when I traveled to meet District Manager Richard Gaddy and his very successful team in Florida. Richard's team had done a masterful job over many years working with varied departments in Florida's State Government to earn a reputation of trusted advisor.

On the first day of my visit, Richard set up review sessions for me with each of his sales managers to talk about their sales teams, followed by individual meetings with each sales representative. With one exception, I met every sales leader in the group that first day. Richard told me, with a smile, that I would meet the last member of his team the next day when I was scheduled to visit one of the largest customers in the District.

I asked Richard if he would be attending the meeting with us. He said, "No, Mike can handle it with you." I asked if I could get a briefing ahead of time. Richard said, "Mike is at the customer site today but left this account plan for you to review," as he handed me a thick packet of information.

That night I read the detailed account plan and was very impressed. It provided a thorough update on everything I needed to know including people, history, applications, opportunities, threats, and current priorities. It clearly laid out who we would meet with the next day, likely issues that would be raised, and our responses. The document blew me away. I went to bed looking forward to our morning meeting.

The next day at 8:00 a.m. sharp, a car pulled up to my hotel and out jumped Mike Willenborg. A big smile on his face, Mike extended his hand and said, "Good morning Rick!" with such gusto that I am sure every bellman within 30 yards jumped. I was beaming as I headed for the passenger's seat.

Mike immediately went on the offensive. "How did yesterday go?" he asked as we settled in for our ride to the customer site. He was questioning me to assess my priorities and reactions to a cast of characters he knew well. Though we had met only minutes before, our conversation was a lively give and take, thanks to the way Mike used open-ended questions to learn more about the latest executive who would soon be introduced to his means of livelihood. He asked if I had any questions about the briefing package he had prepared. His line of questioning was meant to ensure I was ready. But it was clear he had done his homework on me, too.

During the next 30 minutes, he made reference to everything from my education and prior assignments to my volunteer work. And as we went back and forth during the drive, Mike's enthusiasm for his customer and his role in helping his customer succeed came through like a bright light.

"Did you know that we have been identified as one of the top departments in the state for consistently delivering on our plans and staying under our budget projections? And we have been asked to present again this year at the national conference to highlight our best practices for using technology? We're on a roll!" Mike's enthusiasm was palpable.

He loved what he was doing. And I could feel my normally high morning energy level surge even higher to match his.

The customer meetings were successful. Perhaps from Mike's perspective, another "suit" from headquarters had been successfully introduced to his client and had not made a mess of things. From my perspective, I knew I had been given a gift. I had spent time with a gifted and truly powerful person.

The day after I arrived back at the home office I called Richard to talk about the visit. We talked about how the customer visit went but the subject quickly shifted to Mike.

Richard laughed when I described the impact my encounter with Mike had on me. He said, "Welcome to the club." He told me many others had the same reaction to Mike. "He lifts everyone in the office," Richard said.

"About a month ago I asked each sales manager to nominate a member of their team for a District Sales Council," Richard told me. "I wanted us to do a better job sharing best practices across teams. Mike's manager sent Mike and we are still talking about what happened. It was like Mike lit a fuse under his peers. Not only did they share best practices between each other, but they decided to reach out to other districts as well. And I credit Mike. He started a chain reaction. It was great."

It didn't matter that the organization chart showed that Mike sat three levels down from where I sat. In this case, he was Chief. His power came from connecting what he was doing to who he was, and it was infectious.

I have been grateful for that lesson ever since.

# Choices that Enable Viral Engagement

Conventional wisdom says that people with Chief titles are primarily responsible for employee engagement. This thinking fails to account for the impact every single Chief at any level can have on an organization.

Research supports what I have experienced personally, with Mike Willenborg and many other Chiefs along the way—the key is to create the conditions for viral engagement. It starts with the understanding that *any* employee can impact the engagement of *every* employee in a group.

Specifically, research has found that positive emotions spread from person to person in a work environment. An individual's, or group's, emotion plays a strong role in the behavior of an organization. Studies show that positive mood or emotion enhances creative problem solving, cooperation, decision quality, overall performance, the search for creative solutions, and confidence in being able to achieve positive outcomes. One study by Yale researcher Sigal Barsade found that a spread of positive emotion is associated with improved cooperation, decreased conflict, and increased task performance in the workplace. But how does emotion spread?

Emotional contagion works at a less conscious level than cognitive contagion (i.e. the spread of ideas). Scientists believe that emotional contagion is based on automatic processes and physiologic responses, and it works in groups. It is a type of social influence that occurs both consciously and unconsciously. It occurs somewhat behind-the-scenes. The innate behavior of mimicry—the mirroring of facial expressions, body language, speech patterns, and vocal tones—is at play. Once people engage in the automatic process of mimicking, they begin to experience the emotion themselves. The initial process is completely subconscious. Once a person becomes aware of a new emotion, they are at will to change it, but studies show that, more often than not, the new emotion will take hold. Barsade states that "people are 'walking mood inductors,' consciously affecting the moods, and then the judgments and behaviors, of others."

Another study by James Fowler and Nicholas Christakis out of the University of California and Harvard, respectively, found that cooperation also spreads, even among people who are not acquainted. Once again, imitation plays a role in the spread. Our innate mimicking of behavior, just as with emotion, helps to fuel the spread. These researchers found that cooperation spreads not only from person to person, but also from person to person to person to person—up to three degrees of separation. That's an impressive cascade. That's viral engagement.

Engaged employees feel great about giving their all at work. They are disciplined and creative in their chosen craft and team well with others. Their high level of satisfaction comes from working in an environment where they can connect what they do to who they are. They are Chiefs.

Engagement can begin with any individual in any organization. When you are Chief—connecting what you do to who you are—others will notice. They will pick up on your demeanor and behavior and, on a subconscious level, begin to mirror the positive change. This cascade of engagement has the potential to transform your organization. This is the power of being Chief.

In addition to standard and important approaches to increase employee engagement such as regular surveys and decentralization practices, here are 10 additional opportunities for a more comprehensive path to create the conditions for improving employee engagement with the understanding that engagement is contagious and can start from anyone, anywhere in an organization.

**Selection:** Do you hire good team players and hold an expectation that every addition to your team can have an immediate impact on the engagement of current employees?

**Education:** Does your company invest in the soft skills that will enable your employees to be more effective in engaging others?

**Communication:** Do you reinforce verbal and written communication as equally important in engaging others?

**Compensation:** Could you pay a small team bonus for improving engagement scores?

**Recognition:** How could you recognize individuals and teams when new practices are adopted that are generated "bottom up?"

**Promotion:** Do team members know that engagement success is part of the path to promotion?

**Retention:** When people do leave, do you ask about engagement in exit interviews?

**Performance management:** Is engagement a part of performance management discussions?

**Values:** Could engagement language be added to define your organizations values?

**Assessment:** Do you assess for engagement skillsets? When you understand that viral engagement is possible, you have the power to unleash a whole new paradigm in your organization.

Taken together, Values, Insight, Creativity, Discipline,

and Support make up the Power Compass to being Chief. Each individual element overlaps with the others to create a comprehensive and powerful whole. Mike was a living example. Mike never waited for someone to tell him to be Chief. He chose his own direction and followed his own compass. In doing so, Mike was one of the most powerful Chiefs I have ever met. He had more fans and followers than he could ever know, but could certainly count me among them.

Where could your compass take you? Where might it take others?

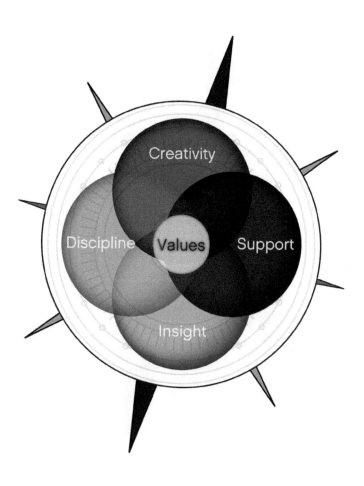

# TWO

# Empower a Team of Chiefs

*Throughout my career I have been called upon to work with groups to fix problems and increase performance. In each circumstance we needed to unlock the power in teams of people. In every situation, we enabled teams of Chiefs with a focus on Discipline, Insight, Support, Creativity, and Values. What follows are five of those stories. Each story begins with background, illustrates how we utilized the five parts of the Compass, and demonstrates how teams of Chiefs at all levels took ownership and drove innovation, productivity, and sustainable growth. Each case ends with a description of the team's amazing business results, enabled by Chiefs and viral engagement.*

## Inspiring Employee Performance

In my 15 years at Unisys, I had moved up from sales trainee to Vice President/General Manager. I had the opportunity to learn from many who were Chief, although few carried that title. With each move, the key to success was supporting employees to be more powerful. But companies vary. What would happen when I was recruited to join an iconic American corporation as the first outsider in their 100-year history to serve as a line sales officer running a part of the company's core business? I was asked to work with a team to turn around a slow-growing $3 billion business unit and now all eyes were on me. Would my lessons transfer?

**Background.** While traveling on a business trip one spring, my eye caught a Fortune magazine cover story with the headline "Could AT&T Rule the World?" The article described the balanced scorecard used at AT&T where almost equal priority was given to attaining financial results, customer satisfaction, and employee satisfaction. The company measured Economic Value Added (EVA), Customer Value Added (CVA), and People Value Added (PVA). It resonated with me immediately. I, too, believed strongly in this approach, having practiced a similarly balanced set of priorities at Unisys for years. The *Fortune* piece gave CEO Bob Allen the credit he was due for doing the right things the right way. Prospects for AT&T were bright. At the time, I was working at the Unisys Corporation, Sperry's successor. I had spent thirteen years rising up through the ranks from my first job as a sales trainee and was fortunate to be mentored by two great business leaders who taught me the importance of relationships in business. They reinforced my already strong beliefs in hard work, honesty, and teamwork.

My future at Unisys was promising, but something wasn't right; I had this nagging feeling of unhappiness because I wanted more. I wanted a bigger stage. When I read the Fortune article, something pulled at me. "I'm going to work at AT&T," I thought aloud. The moment I said it, I knew it was going to happen. "Now I just have to figure out how." I knew that my fellow Columbia classmate Gail McGovern was working there and that gave me a place to start.

I made this vision of working at AT&T my goal. Then I began a two-year campaign to make it a reality. I planned my work and worked my plan, and eighteen months later I was promoted to lead the $500 million Communications Division at Unisys. As the head of my division, I gained valuable experience in the telecommunications industry. I was getting closer to my dream.

At the same time, unbeknownst to me, senior leadership at AT&T had determined it was time for a change. Due to inroads made by competitors MCI and Sprint, discussions were underway as to how to respond to declining market share. When one of its largest clients (GE) replaced AT&T with MCI, leadership decided to take action. Six months later, Gail's peer and Global Services President Jeff Weitzen picked up a phone and said words that he never expected to say, "Rick, would you join AT&T as a Corporate Officer?" He broke with AT&T's long-standing tradition of promoting from within and hired an outsider.

After fifteen years at Unisys, at age 36, I was hired as the youngest corporate officer ever to run a part of AT&T's long lines business unit. I was now leading an organization that generated

$3.3 billion in revenue and I was convinced I had arrived. In reality, I had no flippin' idea what I was walking into.

From my first day on the job, the message was clear: everything—people, resources, processes—needed to be turned around immediately to take market share. It was no short order.

When I arrived, the eastern region was made up of 2,200 very talented sales and support professionals. There was no question that we had the talent to accomplish our goals. However, if a business's culture is the backbone of its success, then it was apparent why AT&T was coming off the rails.

Talented as they were, the employees were demoralized by a surrounding culture that did not understand or value the sales function. In fact, people seemed startled by an expression I used regularly: "Everyone at AT&T has one of two jobs—they either directly support a customer or they support someone who does!" Perhaps due to vestiges of its monopoly history, AT&T was ill equipped to stand out in the market and compete with upstarts MCI and Sprint.

Our people were skilled in dealing with internal requests, but amazingly bad at adapting to the constantly changing world of customers with options. As always in a new assignment, particularly in a turnaround situation, first steps are critical. I was an outsider in a visible position with high stakes and I needed a winning strategy to begin. I turned my focus first to building a new culture. We needed our team to feel powerful. We needed to enable a team of Chiefs.

### First Steps

**Day-One Speeches.** Rumors that an outsider had been

hired to replace the leader of the eastern region had been circulating for weeks prior to my arrival. By the time I sat in my new office for the first time, everyone had lots of questions and they wanted answers. Good or bad, my first impression was going to have an immediate impact on team buy-in. My goals were to make a strong impression, give them certainty that their concerns would be heard, and demonstrate my interest in their individual success as well as the success of our unit. In my first two weeks, I made five speeches and spoke to all 2,200 employees across the entire region.

I can remember how I opened my first town hall meeting.

"Today I have three things I want to accomplish. First and foremost, I want to hear from you to learn about issues and ideas to improve our region's performance with customers, shareowners, and with each other. Second, I want you to know that I have high expectations for your engagement in improving our performance. And third, although almost any topic is on the table for open discussion, I want to be equally clear that one topic is not."

I could see I had their attention now.

I continued, "Specifically, I need each and every one of you to know that I have zero tolerance for any activity that is not aligned with Our Common Bond." AT&T's statement of values was a powerful set of principles that was well understood throughout the employee base:

- Highest Standards of Integrity
- Respect for Individuals
- Dedication to Helping Customers
- Teamwork
- Innovation

"It is the foundation for everything we are doing here."

By reaffirming AT&T's values and establishing them as the foundation for our work rather than simply a plaque on the wall, I set the stage for creating a culture of support. Any organization will benefit from setting such a foundation and revisiting core values again and again.

In all of my presentations I also made it very clear that I recruited AT&T, as opposed to AT&T recruiting me. I told the *Fortune* magazine article story because I wanted everyone to know that I was attracted to AT&T because of its equal focus on financial, customer, and employee success. I also shared that I had selected AT&T in large part due to Our Common Bond and that *how* the company ran was equally important to me. Finally, I let them know I wanted our employees to feel pride in their company as I did. As I stated my expectations, I did so from a place of support rather than higher position. I talked to them rather than at them.

*When you are unsure in a situation, be loose on specifics and firm on generalities to help your team know what's important.*

Overall, the speeches were successful because I held to a very simple rule: Be loose on specifics and firm on generalities. When faced with a generally skeptical and concerned audience and armed with very little specific, firsthand information to share, I connected with my new team by establishing the alignment of my values with those of the company—the intersection of who I was and what I planned to do. This simple rule works.

**The Go Test.** It was a top priority for me to get an early read on my senior team in the region. I needed smart people who could be all-in, people I could trust and who could attract others with the same attributes. When I arrived at AT&T, I found no shortage of data available from the Human Resources Department. In fact, I was overwhelmed by the volume of information contained in the personnel files of every employee in my unit; unfortunately, it was of no value to me.

I once asked a Human Resource manager, "How many of our employees are on performance improvement programs?" He looked at me quizzically as if to say, *why*? According to the files, everyone was doing a terrific job and always had. Looking back, this was my first view into a culture that valued positive internal relationships more than the realities of outside relationships. "Okay," I thought, "I've found my next step."

Experience has taught me that whenever a leader implements a turnaround, he or she will be confronted with three groups of people. The first group, usually about a third of the audience, will generally be enthusiastic about the new direction and will not need a lot of encouragement or explanation to get on board. This is the Go-Go group. A leader is well served to listen to this group and get out of their way.

The second group, usually between a third and a half of the group, will require most of a leader's attention. This is the Go-But group. These individuals want to believe the leader but they need added reassurance, additional information, or time to accept and endorse a new direction. Time taken with this group is well spent.

The third group, usually the smallest, has little, if any, intention of accepting change or willingness to contribute what is required to turn around the organization. This is the No-Go group. A leader can save valuable time if he or she can quickly identify these individuals and give them the opportunity to do something they *do* believe in, either elsewhere within the organization or at another organization. At AT&T, this group was easy to identify. Anytime I heard the expression "Whatever you say Mr. Miller," my antenna went up.

I found the best gauge I had for assessing individuals was using the i3K tool that I learned to use in my first sale to the City of Lynn. I used the i3K tool to evaluate people based on their intelligence, intensity, integrity, and kindness. The i3K criteria can be used to evaluate individuals of any team in any organization. It's a useful barometer for creating effective teams. We learned a lot about our employees' intelligence and intensity when we began to measure and manage our human capital with the same discipline as we did our financial capital, as you will learn later. And we used Our Common Bond values to assess *how* an individual was working as a team member with kindness and integrity. The good news was that kindness was in large supply in the AT&T workforce. I knew I needed smart people who would work hard, and who I could trust. When evaluating intelligence, I was looking for both IQ and EQ—emotional intelligence—a term coined by Peter Sifneos in 1973. EQ is critical to building high-performance teams.

I based my approach to assessing my team on the message contained in Jim Collins' book *Good to Great*: it's *who* first, then *what*. According to Collins, a company's focus (what) may change over time, but if a company has selected great people (who) it will be well positioned for success. My job was to make sure I had the right who. I was looking for those who could be Chief, regardless of their level or title.

**Language.** Language is as much about listening as it is about talking, and it was critical at AT&T. Word choice can be crucial, I've learned, especially in early interactions when you are first building trust. Listening first and then engaging with what the other person says goes a long way in building relationships. Unspoken communication can speak volumes too. I've learned that people try not to say things they don't believe and any awkward silences can tell you a lot.

> *Reading language, spoken and unspoken, including your own, will serve you well if you choose to listen.*

Third, body language can be a very helpful tool, particularly when words and body language are not in alignment. My antenna goes up when someone can't keep eye contact or is constantly shifting in their seat when we are talking.

Finally, using your own body as a gauge for reality is incredibly useful. I realized my body had a remarkable ability to warn me when I was not getting the truth. I learned to never ignore my gut when building relationships.

**Stories.** People remember stories. Facts and figures fade, but a well-structured story can remain fresh in the mind for years to come. I used stories when I arrived at AT&T and one in particular served me better than others.

"Did you know the last branch manager promotion I gave at Unisys was to a sales manager who missed making his revenue quota?" The story caught the attention of my new sales organization. Virtually everyone wanted to know what it took to get promoted, yet they felt the primary objective, if not the only objective, was to make their revenue quota.

I went on. "Why promote someone who missed a number? It was because that sales manager had succeeded in selling a huge account the prior year. He had appropriately focused on completing a very complex installation, ensuring a high level of customer satisfaction. Employee satisfaction had increased on his team and everyone saw that the benefits we promised to the customer became a reality.

Although that sales manager finished the year at 95 percent of his original revenue objective, he also secured a huge new reference account. He understood that customer and employee satisfaction, and the axiom that we do what we say we will do, were critical to sustaining growth. Of course, when I promoted him I told him he better not miss his branch quota the next year and make me look bad! He didn't miss."

*Tell stories that exemplify your message. Stories are remembered while facts and figures fade.*

The explanation of why this individual received a promotion spread throughout my new organization faster than I could have hoped. It communicated how to be Chief in our new culture. It resonated with my team and helped me set the right tone.

**Early Lessons.** While many understand the importance of the right words at the right time, others say talk is cheap. Because I needed positive change, I knew that by entering a large organization with a well-established culture, I would need to provide some strong lessons early in the turnaround.

My first lesson involved promotions and demotions. I decided, as soon as the opportunities presented themselves, that I would promote three people in my organization who were demonstrating both the *what* and the *how* of what I was advocating. I also decided I would demote others if I determined they were not supporting the new direction.

Further, I would not hesitate to fire anyone when it could be proven they had violated Our Common Bond values to the detriment of the company. I intended to maintain AT&T's values as the foundation for our work throughout the organization, as I had promised in my day-one speeches. In hindsight, this strategy had more impact than I expected. In fact, when I completed the review of my four direct reports, it was clear one would be happier elsewhere. In addition, it was a good move to promote two terrific directors, not just one, to vice president, and increase my direct reports to five. The positive impact to the organization was huge.

My second lesson, early on, involved finding opportunities for decentralization. However, in an organization that was rife with centralized control, this was no easy task. AT&T did not have many models for decentralization. It was a big reason why so many people felt powerless. There were plenty of people with titles and power, but not enough recognition of the Chiefs at every level. I wanted to change that.

*Consider promotions and demotions, decentralization, and adopting other's best practices as you get started.*

I consider it synchronicity that the two great leaders I had promoted joined with their three peers and approached me as a team to gain my support for the proposed formation of what they called "The Partnership." They began, "Rick, do you trust us?" before outlining the plan they had put together. My vice presidents were hardworking, smart, ethical, and great with their teams so when they asked me to break the mold and trust their judgment, I knew it could signal the beginnings of our "reinterpreted" organization in a powerful way. I chose to trust their judgment and gave them wide latitude with decision-making. As a team, they were equally outstanding and they delivered incredible results. Better still, they effectively demonstrated that Chiefs existed outside of the company's highest tiers.

My third early lesson involved modeling the behavior required to build relationships with my peer officers, both inside and outside Global Services. It was critical for me to fit in. I was aware of AT&T's well-deserved reputation for rejecting outsiders—office pools wagering how long I would last existed in my own organization. Though I had over one hundred officer peers at AT&T, it was especially crucial for me to be accepted by my two Global Services peers.

Both were seasoned AT&T professionals and had earned the respect of their organizations in the central and western regions. As I pushed my organization to share best practices, I also consciously pushed our group to adopt the best practices (which were plentiful) that existed in their organizations as well. Additionally, I publicly acknowledged both of my peers regularly for their great work and that I was grateful for their support.

Being Chief allowed me to establish my credibility, coalesce a strong team that was ready to work under my leadership (and to lead in their own right), and establish a culture that empowered Chiefs at all levels. The following sections outline other parts of the Power Compass that enabled us to build a team of Chiefs.

### Discipline—Plan Tactics

In my situation at AT&T, particular attention was needed in the area of *planning tactics*. Specifically, customer relations and sales readiness required immediate attention. We needed a finely tuned *disciplined* approach to earn back our credibility, and it had to start from within.

To improve customer relations and counter the aggressive campaigns being waged by MCI and Sprint, we took a number of steps to ensure that we came through for our customers. Every organization faces competition and challenges with customers. The key is to engage Chiefs at all levels to plan tactics.

Together, we incented our workforce to increase the percentage of customers who completed our customer satisfaction surveys and instituted face-to-face debriefing sessions. "Finally, we are measuring the right things!" sales people shared when we announced a system to track customer face time. I have never met a good sales person who liked to spend time in the office.

Next, we developed and implemented a new system to measure customer face time and set goals for increasing compliance. We also instituted rigorous account planning sessions and pushed for customer participation. And finally, we educated our workforce on the higher bar of attaining customer loyalty as opposed to customer satisfaction.

Improving our sales readiness proved to be an equally

challenging issue. In my first full year, all three regions were given level funding that was intended to allow them to avoid a layoff.

The problem was that the prior year's budgets included no money for much-needed sales training. In a very unpopular move, after we scoured the budget to eliminate all waste we could find, I decided to lay off eight percent of my workforce to create enough discretionary money to allow us to establish a solid training budget. It was highly visible—the only layoff in the business segment at AT&T—and it created quite a stir.

The benefit of such a bold move, however, created a lift for those performers who remained, now both better trained and encouraged to see true performance management. We immediately added a specific training focus on higher-margin portions of our product portfolio. We also reorganized and segmented a sales force of generalists into separate relationship management and product specialists to increase accountability. We supported these new positions by developing new compensation plans. When we committed to market-based pay I received a note from a senior sales representative that said simply, "Well done. You get it." We also developed a more consistent performance management system with consequences. In other words we implemented more visibility and accountability, which in turn communicated our disciplined approach—and that we expected the same from our team.

*Consider your opportunity to use disciplined tactics while remaining open to feedback. It is not always easy, but it is critical.*

By actively engaging Chiefs at all levels inside our organization, listening to our customers, and then demonstrating that we would take action on their input, we made consistent progress. With our disciplined approach, we started to earn back much needed credibility with both groups.

## Support—Encourage

When I arrived at AT&T, particular attention was needed in the area of encouragement. Specifically, I needed to break down the walls between levels inside the company in order to encourage honest communication and to unlock the potential of a great group of workers who had come to believe their voices would not be heard. In fact, our biggest challenge was to build trust in and among the employees of the eastern region, a majority of whom had grown up at AT&T.

"This is an alphabet soup!" I was scanning through the collection of letters and levels making up the titles carried by each member of the organization.

Perhaps as a holdover from the days when AT&T employed over a million people, many employees carried a strong sense of hierarchy and were level conscious to the point of distraction. In fact, the managerial practice at the time promoted use of alphabet letters to designate where employees fit on the corporate ladder.

Entry-level positions were designated as A levels and first-level managers as B levels. Senior managers could be designated as either C levels or as district managers. The next level could be referred to as either a D or a division manager. From there it got really confusing. The next level could be referred to as an E level or a director or by adding the term vice president after their job title. Then, there were the five levels of officers, with another set of positional naming rules. At AT&T, titles mattered too much!

The biggest issue I saw was that the employees with lower letters would seldom, if ever, challenge those in positions with higher letters. The underlying assumption was, "Don't make waves with those above you because they could be involved in the committee vote to promote you somewhere down the road. People at higher levels have more power." It was a terrible way to work, resulted in very little honest feedback, and did not encourage or enable the culture I was trying to support. It certainly didn't enable my employees to be Chief. Instead of focusing on strengthening their own power—the power within each and every individual—they viewed power as something to fear. I needed people to speak up!

There was another problem. Culturally, AT&T employees were far more focused on what went on within the company rather than what was going on outside the company. With a history as a regulated monopoly, one can see why. Up until 1982, the government regulated AT&T's prices and profits. There was little incentive for any employee to question the plans that were produced or how they should be implemented, which resulted in a culture of compliance. As a by-product of that culture, these groups simply didn't talk to each other. In a large company with many silos, I needed to encourage employees to reach outside their own organizations and start sharing.

To confirm my suspicion, I reviewed the annual employee satisfaction survey results for the region, focusing on one key question: "Do you think it is safe to say what you believe at AT&T?" I reviewed five years of results and found the highest score ever registered for this question was 39 percent. "So it's likely that six out of ten people wouldn't feel comfortable telling the truth," I thought. I believe that open communication is key to innovation and success. I knew it would come as a shock to the existing culture, but it was time to build a new habit.

So I did the unthinkable. I signed a contract with our competitor, MCI, to set up a toll free number (1-800-SAFE-TO-SAY) that allowed employees to call in and share their thoughts, comments, suggestions, and complaints, which I then received in a weekly report of every call. I regularly addressed the toughest questions submitted and gave my direct answers in town meetings and on employee broadcasts to let everyone know that no question was out of bounds.

> *Consider whom you go to for feedback and how frequently you get it. Could casting a wider net help you help others?*

The program was a huge success. The volume of calls was amazing and the content astonishing. By encouraging open dialogue and ensuring that every voice mattered, we were able to regularly give and receive feedback at all levels. Finally people were talking. Over time people started to ask me questions directly rather than reserve them for the hotline. It was clear that this program increased trust within the organization. We continued to focus on the survey question as a key indicator of future success.

In order to increase trust in your company consider these questions: Does your organization encourage open communication? Do employees feel comfortable to voice their honest opinions? If not, seek to understand the barriers and either eliminate them or create other opportunities for such discussion.

Businesses thrive when employees feel they are trusted, but the conditions must exist or be established for this to occur.

## Creativity and Positive Change

To reinforce the safe-to-say message and encourage everyone to be Chief, we produced hundreds of safe-to-say bumper stickers and put them all over walls in eastern region offices. The positive response led us to expand the campaign. We believed that over time these simple written tools would lead our employees to feel, think, speak, write, and act differently, putting creativity into action. In all, we produced ten bumper stickers to help to create the future and enable more people to be Chief.

At AT&T we created a campaign with bumper stickers that reinforced our goal to be supportive and creative.

We printed the phrase "Born in the East, Adopted by the Segment" to reinforce the need for innovation. We wanted employees to question things they didn't understand and anything they felt was not optimized. We saw an increase in requests for skip-level conversations as well as suggestions about what we could do better.

As a native Bostonian, I regularly referenced words made famous by former Speaker of the House of Representatives, Tip O'Neil, "All Politics are local," to enable local decision making and risk taking. (I admit to altering Tip's actual phrase "all politics is local" on the bumper sticker.)

To counter the prevailing view that hierarchy was a substitute for leadership, we challenged that model directly: "Leadership isn't a Level, it's a State of Mind." By decentralizing as many decisions as possible, employees at lower levels were given greater responsibilities. We encouraged each individual to be Chief.

We printed "Customer Face Time" to reinforce the need for those at the top of our organization to model the behavior we were asking of the team. Our senior leaders saw more customers, and great things happen when you spend time with a customer.

It was important for us to reinforce the message to take responsibility and accountability for what was in our control. "Two ways to catch a bus" acknowledged that things are always changing (the bus is always moving) and if you don't plan (to leave early) you end up wasting valuable energy (running like hell after the bus). We saw agendas arriving days before meetings rather than the day of the meeting, and productivity went up.

We were clear in our definition of success in the eastern region. Without a doubt we wanted to meet and exceed our revenue, profit, and margin plans. We also wanted to be clear that we cared about the well-being of our employees, so we created a bumper sticker that read, "Personal and professional balance." We saw the benefits that occur when employees take their vacation.

We talked a lot about the difference between a satisfied customer and a loyal customer; hence the bumper sticker phrased "Client Loyalty." A loyal customer won't leave you on those occasions when you disappoint. We experienced increasing client loyalty survey scores in spite of occasional hiccups in our operation.

## Do you use creative ways to support others?

"Extraordinary People Drive Extraordinary Results" reinforced the pride we had in our team. We wanted our team members to know we valued them both for who they were and what they did as individuals and as members of our team. People want to know they matter. We could feel the pride in our team rising.

### Celine, Tom, and Creativity

When I first arrived at AT&T, it did not take long for me to hear the name Celine Azizkhan. She was viewed almost universally as an innovative thinker and team builder. She was just the type of Chief I was hoping to find in my new organization. Better yet, she was also responsible for sales growth with new accounts, an area where we needed to show immediate progress. Like all Chiefs, Celine had attracted her own group of top performers. Among her superstars was Tom Cannon, a sales manager who became a Chief in his own right.

The credit for the success of our unit belongs to Chiefs like

Celine and Tom and the *creativity* and viral engagement that each brought to the table.

Celine and Tom had been tasked with leading the newly created acquisition team to win back business AT&T had lost to competitors including MCI, Sprint, Verizon, and other carriers.

Their focus was singular: aggressively pursue large opportunities ($1+ million) inside well-established AT&T sales territories. There was no revenue base to protect, but there were also no meaningful client relationships in place. Instead, the acquisition team was challenged to win back business from clients who had not had any significant relationship with AT&T for many, many years. Relationships needed repair, and senior-level positioning needed to be established. AT&T's value proposition and differentiators had to be well communicated. Sales opportunities had to be discovered or generated. The new sales model required new approaches. In short, Celine and Tom needed to get creative—in how they worked with the customer and with the sales team—if they were going to succeed at their objectives.

I remember one particular sales meeting with Celine and her team early in my new assignment. Celine jumped straight to work. "The way I see it, we have three primary challenges," she began. "Access, of course, is the first. AT&T's relationships with these companies have fallen by the wayside—if they ever existed at all—so we've got our work cut out for us in gaining access to key decision makers and influencers."

Tom nodded. Neither was too concerned. As sales leaders, the two of them had all been in this position before; it was routine, even comfortable. Plus, the internal selling responsibilities would amp up their focus. "It would be nice to come in strong,"

Tom added, "Bring something sweet to the table."

"Exactly!" Celine replied. "We've got to get special pricing and flexible terms from the strategic pricing organization, and maybe even set a few precedents."

Both nodded in agreement at her statement. AT&T's strategic pricing organization was a tightly closed purse of Dickensian proportions. Setting new precedents would be tough. "And, of course, we have our two sets of teams," Celine said, referring to their second challenge.

As the Sales VP, Celine had the dual responsibility to 1) position the acquisition team within each region as complementary to the already established in-region sales teams and 2) position the acquisition team as the sales lead.

Tom and Celine's success hinged on building rapport between the two teams and earning the confidence and trust of the in-region AT&T team. In many situations, the acquisition team was a welcome teammate, but in some cases, they were viewed as a trespasser. When welcomed, the team quickly gained traction and achieved success. When met with resistance, they spent more time building and strengthening internal relationships, and sales were delayed. The success of both the acquisition team and the in-region sales teams required everyone's buy-in.

"EVA, CVA, PVA," Celine said, "Economic, Customer, and People Value Added. As always, we haven't succeeded until we've mastered all three."

Achieving sales success was paramount; the numbers had to be there. If the acquisition team reached sales goals while also garnering internal and client praise, the mission would be accomplished. This was the third challenge, and where Celine's leadership, and in particular her creativity, would prove so crucial. She was an expert at building internal relationships and removing sales obstacles. As her direct report, Tom was given the latitude to manage a sales program, make personnel decisions, and execute on sales strategies and tactics. In other words, Celine empowered Tom to be Chief.

Creativity was one of Celine's key strengths. The way she felt and thought was aligned with what she said and did. The energy that she applied to both was palpable. And it spread. Celine always encouraged new, thoughtful approaches. "We need new ideas. Share your wackiest approaches." Then she added, "after you've done some due diligence." Ready, shoot, aim was not a recipe for success under her watch. She expected well thought out positioning and sales strategies, but she was open to input from everyone on the team. The sense of creative empowerment was real and rewarding. Celine made everyone feel important to any sales success. The experience, and seeing the impact it had on the team, resonated with Tom in a profound way.

There were an obvious energy and buzz that came with being part of the team. Confidence soared, especially as the acquisition team far exceeded revenue goals. Tom, in particular, felt profoundly impacted, conditioned to take on the toughest challenges, and, of course, taught to always look for a creative solution. When Tom's energy increased to match Celine's, he became more powerful and he influenced everyone around him, not from fear, but more by inspiration.

Celine was an all-in manager, totally engaged thinking all the time. She demonstrated imagination, thoughtfulness, and openness to new ideas. Mindful of the words that she spoke to her team (and holding her actions in alignment with what she said), Celine created space for creativity while reinforcing the values core to the organization (and her own). You keep credibility when you do what you say and say what you do. Alignment of those things was powerful. Celine taught Tom to generate energy, optimism, enthusiasm, and results. Tom became a Chief who enabled others to be Chief, too.

### Insight—Be Present

Much like the cynicism that met Celine and Tom at times, I was met with broad cynicism when I joined AT&T as well. Many outsiders in other divisions at lower levels before me had come and gone. The size and scope of the job was like nothing I had experienced before and this was my first job in fifteen years outside Sperry/Unisys. It was critical for me to take it one day at a time. In fact, it was critical for me to take one moment at a time to learn all that was available at each step along the journey. It would have been a mistake to multitask when I had the opportunity to fully engage with employees who wanted me to give them my undivided attention—something they had not always received from prior outsiders. One story that came to my early attention at AT&T was the practice of a prior "outsider" to work on his email while he conducted annual performance reviews for his direct reporting team members. I valued my time with my team and gave them my full attention at every opportunity. In hindsight, the choice to *be present* set the tone for growth and was a critical part of the plan to build a team of Chiefs.

### Values

I was lucky that the company values outlined in Our Common Bond, which had been part of AT&T for decades, were generally well understood by a large percentage of the employee base. I had never worked in a company where values were such a visible part of company culture. It was critical to the growth of the organization that I reinforced these values in day-to-day discussions. Integrity, respect, teamwork, innovation, and customer focus became my mantra. I was also lucky that Our Common Bond values mirrored my own strongly held personal values of truth, service, equality, and connection.

## Business Results: Growth

While the actions outlined above are provided as an overview of selected leadership activities, they are in no way intended to substitute for the daily work of a team of Chiefs who worked hard and smart for three years delivering results for shareowners, customers, and for each other. Our employees not only bought into the new culture, they adopted it into their work habits and modeled the same behavior to our customers. We became a powerful team. We benefited from viral engagement as being Chief cascaded throughout all levels. As a result of our high-performing culture, we stopped losing market share and gained significant share from our competitors. Our revenue growth rate more than tripled from 4.8 percent at $3.3 billion when I arrived, to a three-year compound annual growth rate (CAGR) of 15.6 percent and a revenue total of $5.1 billion.

Our customer satisfaction survey results similarly went from last of the three regions to first. Our employee engagement survey results went from last of the three regions to first and we scored over 50 percent on the safe-to-say question, which we understood was an all-time high for a similarly sized unit in the company.

We also experienced a phenomenon I called "noses against the glass." In New York City during the holiday season, department stores create colorful, almost magical displays in their windows. It is common for people to simply stop in front of these windows to admire what's inside. Children can be seen pressing their faces against the glass, wanting to get closer to the magic on the other side. When I started at AT&T, I shared with many that our goal was to create that same special feeling in the eastern region and that others in the company would want to join our magic. Together, we succeeded.

**Your Turn.** By now you are familiar with some of the ways in which I have utilized the elements of being Chief to build a team of Chiefs. The choices we made regarding each element drove our success. Next, please take some time to consider your own choices, using the following questions:

- When are you able to have the insight to be present? What effect does it have on you?
- When does your ability to write help you create the future?
- How do you use discipline to plan tactics?
- When do you use support to encourage?
- How have you seen these elements lead to group success? In what other ways could they be used to drive personal growth?

## Taking On Friendly Fire in a Multinational

Bernie Ebbers went to jail. But years earlier he was the CEO of MCI WorldCom, my archenemy in the telecom market. Growing a worldwide business is tough, but when you are facing illegal activity from your primary competitor and friendly fire from inside your company it can feel nearly impossible.

As I approached the end of our third year at AT&T, our unit was consistently gaining market share in the east, and best practices were being shared among Chiefs at all levels more extensively than ever before across Global Services. At the same time, this would become the first time I faced threats from inside my own company.

**Background.** When AT&T hired a proven and decisive leader with a strong technology background to replace Bob Allen as new CEO, change accelerated at the company. Mike Armstrong inherited a company that was ill equipped to deal with the competitive threats posed in the business market by MCI and Sprint or in the consumer market by the Regional Bell Operating Companies (RBOC) like Verizon. Mike began a well-publicized acquisition phase and added people and other assets to compete on all fronts. Part of that acquisition phase included the purchase of Teleport, a company run by AT&T alum Bob Annunziata. Mike asked Bob to run the business segment at AT&T. Shortly after Bob was named, I met with both Bob and Mike.

Mike opened the meeting with news that made me want to shout out loud. "Rick, you've done a great job in the Eastern Region and Bob and I think you can do more to help the company.

We'd like you to become Global Services President." I was tasked to lead a 10,000-person organization that generated close to $12 billion in worldwide revenue and report to Bob directly.

I knew that leading a Global unit was going to be a challenge, but I had a compass. As always, I knew the key would be to build a team of powerful Chiefs. But there were many things I could not know.

Mike Armstrong clearly had his hands full when he took over at AT&T. Though there was no shortage of company insiders around him, Mike was looking to shake things up and made it clear that changing the company's culture was a top priority. When he arrived, Mike found a culture that was internally focused and slow to react to market changes. That needed to change, and fast.

In order to balance the money he was spending on acquisitions in the consumer market, Mike raised expectations on the business segment—our new benchmark for success was MCI. These expectations, coupled with his desire for quick turnaround results added pressure on all to perform. Bob responded by adding a layer of management between himself and his direct reports, selecting an AT&T veteran to run the business segment. That meant I would have a new boss.

I had been lucky that Jeff Weitzen was my first boss. I felt that he always had my back and trusted me to be Chief. I was not so lucky with my new boss. When I got the new job, I couldn't move past the fact that my new boss and I didn't see eye to eye.

When I took over Global Services, I believed I knew how to turn the unit around. My team and I utilized many of the first steps that worked so well in the eastern region. While MCI offered a unique set of challenges during this time period, dealing with the "friendly fire" that was coming from inside AT&T was making my job difficult. A series of announcements seemed to signal a dismantling effort that was making everyone nervous. How could I build a team of Chiefs when everyone thought the organization was being taken apart?

Here is how we applied the Power Compass.

## Discipline—Adjust

Based on my recent experience, I felt I had a good idea about many of the challenges we would be facing. I learned quickly, however, that we needed to pay particular attention to the area of *adjusting*.

To my new boss's credit, when he took over the business segment, he advocated for reasonable assignments for his unit and he accurately carried the message that MCI's aggressive pricing seemed inconsistent with their quarterly reports of improving margins. Unfortunately, nobody was listening. The business segment was burdened with irrational growth targets and expense cuts that needed to be distributed among the business sub-segments. For reasons known only to my boss, he chose to place a disproportionately high level of the expense cut load on Global Services.

Just one month into my new assignment, we got hit with our first big blow: "Global Services needs to absorb a 50 percent headcount reduction. We're going to start with a voluntary separation program that's open to everyone." I read the email and felt my heart sink. We could not restrict who participated in any way and that meant I was going to lose some of my best people. In fact, that's just what happened.

Separately, Mike Armstrong had determined AT&T needed a new strategy for a segment of our largest worldwide accounts. It felt like jab number two when I learned that Mike had decided to offer these accounts to a new joint venture with partner British Telecom. We now needed to convince a number of my Global Service customers, and the employees who served them, that joining this new, separate entity would be preferable to remaining with AT&T.

Next, when a decision was made to transition account control from Global Services to the AT&T Solutions unit for all outsourcing contracts, I felt like a punch had landed. I had worked hard to convince my account managers that teaming with another business unit would be in everyone's best interest.

They had trusted me. This new direction would have a major negative impact on my team's earnings. I was disappointed.

Finally, when my boss chose to move smaller Global Service accounts to another unit, I felt like a knockout had been delivered. In this case, customers would need to adjust to a reduced level of service and build new relationships with a new group of AT&T leaders, creating a great opportunity for a competitor to step in.

All four challenges hit my Global Services team during our first quarter together, before we had a chance to build any real momentum. One sales rep summed up what many of us thought, "What are they smoking?"

Any one of these adjustments would have been challenging for a unit to absorb. Together, they signaled to the entire organization that Global Services was being taken apart. It did not take long for rumors to start circulating that my boss was behind the effort to dismantle the organization. We needed to pull ourselves off the mat and deliver. What could we do to adjust and convince our team members to step up and rekindle their power?

**R3.** We chose to dramatically simplify our management focus. We used the symbol R3 to represent the singular focus of our organization. R3 was shorthand for the statement: "We will deliver Results for 3 groups of important people (customers, shareowners, and employees) by displaying unparalleled levels of excellence in 3 areas (teamwork, innovation, and speed)." In our time of crisis, we felt we needed to unite our remaining workforce behind a simplified version of what AT&T had always stood for: CVA, EVA, PVA (Customer, Economic, and People Value Added) and Our Common Bond. Every action we took as a management team (meeting agendas, reviews, recognition events, etc.) needed to directly relate to R3 so we could stay focused on a clear and simple mission that everyone understood.

> *Could a simplified symbol*
> *help you and your group?*

**Disciplined human resources management.** It might seem counterintuitive to increase the rigor and discipline of human resource management at the same time that employees were dealing with layoffs, voluntary retirement, and massive transfers. But in fact, increasing our focus on people metrics was a critical part of our success during this difficult period.

Our objective was to build a sustainable competitive advantage through our people. We needed our team to feel powerful. Our major adjustment was to begin to measure and manage our human capital with the same discipline and intensity that we used to measure financial capital. In a company-wide culture that was growing more and more top-down, I wanted to let these individuals know that they could still be Chief regardless of their level.

As the old adage says, "If it is important, you measure it." By increasing the discipline around human resources, we not only improved our business prospects but we also sent a clear message to our remaining employee base. We showed them that they were important.

## Does your group measure "people metrics" with the same granularity as other metrics?

### Support—Question

Many in the organization were looking to me to see if I would question some of the decisions that were being made by those above me to split up the business unit just as I was taking over the helm of the ship. I did. I also knew that to build a team of Chiefs, I needed to question my team and be willing to listen to what they told me. I had to create and encourage a dialogue with all levels. It's what real Chiefs do.

One of AT&T's biggest cultural challenges during this tumultuous time was the fact that many employees still retained the expectation of lifelong employment. As part of their belief in that anachronism, employees offered the company almost heroic levels of effort and sacrifice.

At that first town meeting, a longtime employee asked me

why the company expected his loyalty when it was clear to him the company had no loyalty toward him. I recognized that he was really asking about the nature of the new definition of the agreement AT&T was offering its workforce. I took this as an opportunity to outline a new contract. It was a big change for AT&T, as it is for so many organizations. The decision to rewrite, revise, or even re-do employee contracts is not one that is made lightly. In fact, I've found that it takes a lot of introspection and honest assessment before an organization even realizes that it's time to move down that path.

Simply stated, I offered that it was the responsibility of all employees to continuously learn and constantly improve their performance. It was the shared responsibility of the employee and the company to increase the market value of each employee, with both parties "putting our money where our mouth was." This made every employee more difficult to retain. As we encouraged employees to see themselves as more marketable, our employees could choose to commit to the new contract, or they could walk away. As Chiefs, they had my respect either way. It was also the company's responsibility to work harder every day to earn the right to retain the services of an increasingly valuable workforce.

### *Is there an opportunity for you to be clearer with members of your team about the informal contract in your group or organization?*

Looking back, one thing that made this new contract believable was the commitment we made as an organization to learning. We asked our employees what they needed, and listened to what was said. We developed an extensive set of offerings for employees in common functions that voluntarily joined together as learning communities. In spite of budget reductions, extensive learning plans were developed and funding was set aside for training and required travel. The learning communities played a major role in increasing the communication that held the workforce together and greatly supported our new contract.

### Insight—Be Accepting

After getting the good news that I was being promoted into my dream job, it seemed like all my good luck turned to bad luck. It was clear to everyone that I did not have the support of my new boss. It was important for me to question the decisions that were being made above me to show my team that I was willing to fight. At the same time, after pushing back for a while, it was critical for me to *accept* decisions that I could not change.

Personally, I learned a lot about myself as I moved past the frustration phase into an action phase. And yes, at times I felt powerless. Once I released the initial anger I felt toward my boss, I was freed to more clearly focus on the many choices still available to me to support my team. That insight allowed me to lead a team of talented people through the friendly fire. In hindsight, the choice to *be accepting* also set the tone for growth and was a critical part of the plan to regain my power and enable a team of Chiefs.

## Robin, Mike, and Insight

As I moved past my own frustration at things beyond my control, I had the opportunity to fill my previous position. I chose to promote an amazing Chief for the assignment—Robin Hoppe. Robin had a reputation for doing the right things in the right way. In one of the first acts in her new assignment, she had to develop a forecast for future sales. She was fortunate that her financial partner, Mike Kalousis, was growing into his role as Chief. But with the illogical behavior we were seeing in the marketplace, and in our own company, many of our strongest Chiefs found themselves second-guessing their decisions.

The success our organization achieved, in spite of the unethical behavior all around us, is a testament to the insight of the many people involved who were able to look inside for answers. This was an area where Robin excelled, and while it is clear that Robin influenced Mike, there is also no doubt that Mike played his own role enabling our viral growth of Chiefs in the cascade.

When Robin took over responsibility for the eastern region sales organization, Mike was her CFO and he had responsibility for revenue forecasting on a monthly and quarterly basis in addition to running the sales operations function. Robin and Mike submitted their monthly and quarterly revenue forecast as part of a monthly operating review. Mike had a four-year track record of never missing a revenue forecast—something that was a huge point of pride for him. But in their first forecast together, Mike and Robin missed their revenue forecast "by a country mile."

It was a time of great change in the telecommunications market as WorldCom (Bernie Ebbers) was dropping prices dramatically. Aggressive pricing set new "lows" with each deal, and Mike and Robin felt like they were in an elevator with no ground floor. Everything kept going down.

Mike, in particular, was struggling with the failure. Not only had Mike never missed a forecast, his forecast accuracy during the previous four years had a margin of error of less than 2 percent. He felt his power, his weight in the organization, came from his ability to forecast accurately. He would learn, though, that power doesn't come from status or even skills. When Mike found out how badly they had missed the forecast, he immediately felt the need to do a deep dive to understand and explain the situation to Robin and the leadership team. He was concerned that the forecasting process that had been so accurate in the past was now flawed. More than that, the miss felt personal. After Robin heard Mike out, she said simply, "Well, let's figure out what happened."

Robin handled the entire situation admirably. She never got rattled. Instead, she sought to understand each of her direct report's method and point of view on their forecast. Robin scheduled follow-up calls and sessions with each Sales Center Leader to go through their forecast in detail, similar to how she and Mike handled the monthly operating review with more emphasis on specific customers, opportunities, and deal pricing.

The conversations focused on determining the difference between the initial opportunity assessment and the final negotiated deal. As Robin said to Mike, "Ultimately the question is if you knew that the deal was being priced lower than what we originally expected, why was there no update to the forecast reflecting the new pricing?"

The respect and admiration that Robin cultivated with Mike and the rest of the team made it possible for her to ask such direct questions without putting anyone on the defensive. She had an astonishing level of credibility and insight that derived from the transparency with which she handled all her business dealings.

Whether the situation was good or bad, Robin would always address the elephant in the room. She handled business problems admirably because she always sought to understand others' points of view and offered advice and assistance to the team without accusations. Her insight was impactful, and she shared it generously. She would jump in to support her team and would offer up her own ideas and experiences so that others would learn.

Robin's ability to adapt to change had a big influence on Mike. As he learned to be more flexible, his influence with sales leaders increased and he became a more powerful leader in his own right.

Robin handled the entire ordeal in a calm, cool manner once again. Her ability to know what questions to ask displayed her insight, and her strong command of the entire process displayed her ability as a Chief. "We win as a team and lose as a team," she'd say. "Never lose a deal alone."

In the end, Robin and Mike put together a thorough analysis to explain the miss. The marketplace was so fluid in pricing that even if they updated the forecast, it would still have been too late in some circumstances to recover effectively. Robin stood by Mike's side throughout the entire episode in full support, showing ownership and leadership. Through her actions, she instructed that how a leader reacts in difficult situations is often the most important thing. In times like these, a person's character is truly evident. Mike learned that leadership is not a level; it is a state of mind. He has been leading this way ever since.

## Values

While, thankfully, Chiefs like Robin and Mike acted in ways that were consistent with AT&T's stated values, my personal experience was that Our Common Bond was no longer consistently present at the top of the company. In particular, some said the pressure that Mike Armstrong put on members of the senior team to match MCI's "superior" business results took its toll on relationships among the corporate officers.

Thankfully, that was not the case in our unit.

When everything in an organization seems to be changing, it is important to emphasize that a group's values do not. Commonly held values are the foundation of a group's power. With all the shifts planned for Global Services, our continued focus on the visibility of Our Common Bond served us well. It allowed us to stay focused on the mission at hand with the understanding that how we worked together would not change. Personally, it was important for me to work in a place where my strong belief in the truth was supported. In hindsight, once Global Services employees had time to understand the rationale for tough internal decisions that were out of their control, I believe they responded well in large part because they knew their direct management would always tell them the truth.

## Business Results: Growth

As it turned out, we were all chasing Bernie Ebbers' MCI

mirage—it was years later that we learned the results reported by MCI during that period were bogus and Mr. Ebbers went to jail. Despite an incredible amount of distractions from friendly fire and irrational pricing in the market, the powerful Chiefs on the Global Services team still managed to excel—our simplified R3 focus, our disciplined human resource management approach, and our open communication style all combined to unlock an amazing amount of employee productivity in a stress-filled environment.

In spite of all our challenges, we built a comeback that more than doubled our growth rate and added close to a billion dollars in revenue to AT&T. We improved our customer loyalty scores to all-time highs, and our employee-focused strategy also delivered outstanding results. Our employees told us loudly and clearly in the employee satisfaction survey that our actions had earned their support despite market madness and friendly fire. In just one year, employee scores for unit leadership's ability to meet future challenges increased by 40 percent while overall employee satisfaction increased by 19 percent. Our scores increased in several other important areas as identified in the following chart [on the following page].

## AT&T Employee Engagement Results

| ENGAGEMENT ELEMENT | AT&T INCREASE | GLOBAL SVC INCREASE |
|---|---|---|
| Leaders capable of meeting challenges | 11 | 40 |
| Satisfaction with training | 6 | 41 |
| Continuous learning is promoted | 2 | 30 |
| AT&T offers long term career opportunities for me | 13 | 32 |
| I would recommend AT&T as a good place to work | 11 | 30 |
| Unit management will act on problems identified in the survey | 9 | 29 |
| I am NOT currently considering leaving AT&T | 10 | 28 |
| Overall Employee Satisfaction | 5 | 19 |

Employee engagement metrics are crucial to understanding how to best optimize human capital. This is especially true during challenging times as shown by results from AT&T's Global Services engagement survey.

*PricewaterhouseCoopers formally recognized our human resource strategy when we received a national award from Linkage, Inc. for human resource innovation.*

We did, however, miss the corporate revenue objective for that year—the one that was based on an MCI growth-rate benchmark that was proven later to have been the results of cooked books.

## Changes and Vulnerability

One of my biggest challenges during this period was to find a way to personally connect with a workforce that increasingly saw any corporate officer as part of the problem. While we had a large number of people choose to act as Chiefs, the uncertainties of the pending reorganizations caused many others to hold back. Some were just frustrated.

Our entire organization was undergoing massive change. Members of our leadership team had widely distributed copies of Spencer Johnson's *Who Moved My Cheese* to help people view change in more positive terms. The book's simple messages hit a chord with our employees and they responded to its key principles:

- Change happens – They keep moving the cheese.
- Anticipate change – Get ready for the cheese to move.
- Monitor change – Smell the cheese often so you know when it is getting old.
- Adapt to change quickly – The quicker you let go of old cheese, the sooner you can enjoy new cheese.
- Change – Move with the cheese.
- Enjoy change – Savor the adventure and enjoy the taste of new cheese.
- Be ready to change quickly and enjoy it again – They keep moving the cheese.

Chiefs at all levels held town hall meetings to encourage frank and open discussions about change. Conversations were often heated.

In one particular town hall meeting an employee asked me if I understood the impact of losing health care benefits when a family member had cancer. Implied in the question was an assertion that as an officer, I was unaffected by the potential implications of layoffs and voluntary packages. The question also put the issue of separation of personal and professional issues front and center. It gave me an opportunity to share a personal vulnerability I had purposefully kept hidden.

*Could you bring more of your personal life to the professional setting? If you did, could it encourage others to do the same as a way to connect?*

Although I never attempted to hide the fact I had diabetes, I made a very different decision about how to manage the visibility of my bout with cancer. Years ago, as a high-potential new leader at Sperry, I learned I had a malignant tumor that needed immediate surgery. I did not share this with anyone at work. I kept it a secret because I feared it would hold me back from moving up the corporate ladder. Other than my secretary and my boss, no one in the company ever knew.

During that town hall meeting it struck me: "This is a great opportunity." After I addressed the questioner's specific issue with information about transition health care options that would continue his family coverage, I took a chance. I deliberately put myself into a vulnerable position as a way to connect to my team. Brené Brown, a sociological research professor and author of the *New York Times* bestsellers, *The Gifts of Imperfection* and *Daring Greatly*, has created a movement that is changing the way we think about vulnerability, a topic she studies.

Although I may not have realized it at the time, by exposing my vulnerability I was actually being more courageous than when I tried to muscle though my professional life without opening up about my past cancer bout. You could have heard a pin drop when I said, for the first time publicly, "I am a cancer survivor and I know how important health care coverage can be."

The benefits of openly acknowledging both the uncertainty of the future and the link between our personal and professional lives was huge. Not only did I demonstrate that the truth is always safe-to-say, but with the subsequent increase in employees who chose to reach out proactively to engage me in conversation thereafter, it was clear the animosity that had been coming my way as an officer was gone. My vulnerability in fact made me more powerful, and it made my team more powerful. A lot more people chose to join me in being Chief that day.

**Your Turn.** Can you recall a time when you and a team had to navigate a difficult situation in your personal or professional life? Please take some time to consider your own choices and their impact on building a team of Chiefs, using the following questions:

- How do your feelings impact the power of your creativity?
- Do you have the insight to be accepting? What is the result?
- How do you use discipline to adjust?
- What support do you give that allows others to openly question?
- How have you seen these elements lead to group success? In what other ways could they be useful to drive personal growth?

## Growing in a Startup

"The problem is they have no idea why we are even here," I said to the other members of my new senior leadership team at Opus 360. "They aren't just skeptical, they don't think there's a problem at all." Most of our young employees believed the company was already on its way to a successful initial public offering (IPO), the first step in a process that would make them all rich. They already felt powerful, but what they didn't know is that real power doesn't come from status. Why did they need us old folks, a senior leadership team that had been put in place to steer the company in its exciting course? We needed to help them understand what being Chief really meant. Especially once NASDAQ crashed.

**Background.** With the coming of the new economy, many of my friends had jumped out of corporate life to participate in the Internet Revolution. The Internet was changing everything. Startup companies with little or no revenue were getting attention and regularly raising tens to hundreds of millions of dollars through IPOs. Many of my peers were changing their game during this time of unequalled opportunity. I was intrigued by the new economy, by new ways of doing business, and by the opportunity to work at a startup with a group of talented people. One such peer was my friend John Drew. When John called me to suggest that I consider a job as president, COO, and member of the board of directors of a startup company named Opus 360, where he was on the board, the timing was right.

"We need a 'gray hair,'" John said, laughing. My job would be to serve as the seasoned old guy and run all aspects of operations of a small, 200-employee organization. My other job was to partner with CEO Ari Horowitz on the upcoming road show that preceded our planned IPO.

Horowitz and Carlos Cashman started Opus, a company specializing in innovative workforce solutions, in 1998. Both entrepreneurs were innovative visionaries who had a common view of the future of human capital and had a track record of success. Ari and Carlos were convinced the future belonged to the independent worker.

They saw a world where full-time employment would decline rapidly as companies increased the percentage of their temporary workforce. At the same time, workers would gain great flexibility and more control over their career. These project-based workers would act as free agents, capable of filling the needs of an organization by arriving just in time to begin a project and leaving the company when the project was completed. Opus was founded to "change the way the world works."

This view of the world created several business opportunities. First, an exchange, or marketplace, needed to be created to bring together buyers with specific projects (companies) and individual sellers with specific skills (free agents). The company had initiated a major software development effort with the assumption that standards could be established among many constituents.

Second, an opportunity was created to attract free agents and to market products and services directly to them, supporting their independent lifestyle. Opus had already begun an aggressive advertising campaign to publicize this opportunity to a dispersed, independent community across the country.

Third, increased reliance on traditional staffing companies and temporary agencies would create an opportunity for automated solutions to handle the increased workload and improve the quality of the matches. This would require another major software development effort, in addition to a marketing and sales effort to get between staffing companies and their existing end user clients.

My first month at Opus was a blur of activity and excitement: meeting a new team of people; watching where, how, and when the team worked together; listening intently to learn about opportunities and challenges faced by each group; meeting with our early adopter customers; and building relationships with my new boss and fellow board members. As always, I was focused on building a team of Chiefs. And I used many of the same tactics that served me at AT&T—specifically, the day-one speech, team assessment, and early lessons, which are powerful tools that can be utilized in any organization.

We had the good fortune of being able to quickly recruit five strong Chiefs to join in senior positions at Opus. In hindsight, we had a senior management team that would have been the envy of any company, startup or established. Seasoned and savvy leaders hailing from AT&T, IBM, Cendant, Computer Associates, and ADP all brought exceptional experience to a group of employees who had no idea how badly they needed it. It was clear to me shortly after I arrived in February of 2000 that although all of our three business opportunities had potential, we would need to focus on developing software to automate the interactions between companies and their staffing partners. A startup like Opus, with only $1 million in annual revenue, would not be able to continue to spend millions each month to pursue all three opportunities. This was particularly true if it had plans to go public. Understandably, many employees were concerned about new players scaling back their established plans. I heard the rumblings: "The old guy doesn't get it."

On March 10, 2000 it became clear to everyone that our real struggles were just getting started. The NASDAQ crash had begun and the new economy was in trouble. A new norm that revolved around the uniform belief in the over-valuation of the Internet sector quickly spread. As steady declines were reported daily across both NASDAQ and the New York Stock Exchange, our plans to take the company public were now very much in doubt. Early investors were nervous. Early adopter customers who had been excited about working with a dotcom were now seriously concerned about doing business with a dot-bomb. Our young employees that had become accustomed to constant forward momentum were now looking for reassurance. "Maybe the old guy has an idea."

After March 10 it was clear to everyone that we needed to take another look at everything, including our strategies for customers, competitors, costs, capital, and our community of investors and partners. With the bubble burst, life would have to be very different. As I would learn over time, the good news was we had an incredible millennial-based workforce to face the challenge. As Chiefs, our senior team needed to stabilize our inexperienced team and show them how to weather this difficult time. It was key to enable our workers to regain their power. Here's how we used the Power Compass to do that.

## Discipline—Envision

Thankfully, in the midst of all that was changing around Opus, we could rely on the foundational vision that Ari and Carlos put in place when they founded the company: "We change the way the world works."

As a result, our employees were able to *envision* the "why" behind our work. They were also able to use that compelling idea for necessary solid footing as virtually everything, other than our values, changed.

Specifically, as we fashioned a new reality internally to match a quickly changing set of market dynamics, it was critical to:

- Increase frequency of employee meetings
- Increase senior management visits to key customers
- Increase communication with partners and investors
- Accelerate our expense reduction plan and margin improvement program
- Intensify our performance management plan
- Re-focus our management dashboard to only the most critical metrics
- Shift our focus to the corporate market and move resources from our free agent business
- Benchmark employee compensation and benefit information
- Set up employee development plans
- Work with our financial advisors to revise our IPO plans

All of these changes were aided by our team's ability to envision a compelling picture of the future.

*Can you crisply define the mission for your group or organization? Can the team you work with define the mission equally well?*

## Mary Anne, Dana, and Discipline

You would think that a company focused on a new vision for how a human resource model could change the way the world works would be disciplined in its operations. While it was clear when I arrived at Opus that one of the company's strengths was a gifted set of individuals in our human resource department, it was also clear that the chaos of a startup was taking its toll on this talented team of Chiefs. Luckily, one of the savvy leaders recruited to join our team and head HR was AT&T veteran Mary Anne Walk. Mary Anne was not only an expert in the field of human resources, but she was also a certified Master Coach and Chief. Soon after her arrival, our human resource department began operating at a new level.

Prior to the dotcom crash, Dana Zohar, one of the original Chiefs at Opus, and five other HR professionals, were working for Mary Anne. Each brought different skillsets and strengths to their individual roles. Dana's role was that of the lead generalist— essentially, Mary Anne's deputy director. Dana played her own role enabling our viral growth of Chiefs in the organization and beyond. The rest of the team all helped to oversee the delivery of recruiting, benefits, compensation, payroll, organizational design, and employee relations.

In true dotcom fashion, Opus' workforce scaled from 30 to 300 employees in just two years. During this time, the size of the HR team did not grow on par with the rest of the workforce; as a result, the team was incredibly busy and stretched. Being the natural go-to person for HR issues of any topic, "Hey, are you busy?" became the official tagline of Dana's workday. She was constantly interrupted with questions, tasks, and larger concerns that needed addressing.

It didn't take long before Dana's day was filled with putting out small fires. Some days it seemed that it was all she could do to keep her head above water, largely because Dana would rarely turn away those who darkened her doorway. She was selfless in her willingness to serve the organization, but it came at a high cost. Dana's strategic projects were not getting completed as a result of the perpetual interruptions.

One day, Mary Anne took it upon herself to hang a note on Dana's office door that read:

> *Because I am busy in my office, it appears that I am available to speak with you, but I am actually busy working on your behalf. Please see Ruth to get time on my calendar.*
>
> *Thanks!*
>
> *—Dana*

Initially, the note felt like an ego blow. Dana worried it could infer to her colleagues that she was not capable of managing her time. But then something incredible happened: no one interrupted her. Those who came looking for Dana respected her time and focus by scheduling themselves into her day, rather than simply walking into it. The impact of this small change went far beyond an improved ability to focus. When Dana did meet with her colleagues to discuss issues, she was able to offer her full attention and investment, which made the meetings more effective. Most importantly, Dana was able to get back on track with all of her strategic projects and better manage her work/life balance.

Mary Anne's note was a lesson in discipline, support, and encouragement. It was unspoken—demonstrated through quiet action. She didn't tell Dana to prioritize her time better; instead she valued Dana's time by taking action to defend it.

Mary Ann showed Dana that too much of a good thing can be a problem. She acknowledged that Dana's intentions were right, but pointed out that such selflessness was doing more harm than good. More than anything, Mary Ann increased Dana's power by helping her establish disciplined boundaries.

Mary Anne is a true Chief who often coaches by showing rather than telling. In this case, she taught that discipline isn't a matter of simply reigning yourself in or holding your nose to the grindstone. Rather, discipline sometimes requires that you push back on others before you can help them or provide the best level of service possible. Discipline requires adjustment.

## Support—Model

Beyond Mary Anne, we all needed to focus on *modeling*. As I indicated earlier, the best news for Opus was that we had an excellent, experienced senior team to model. The initial reaction: "Who are these old guys and why do we need them?" quickly changed to "Maybe these guys can help us find a way out of this mess." Our senior team walked the walk, talked the talk, and showed the way to a great group of people who were only short on experience, while listening to our workforce to ensure we were all on the same page.

Through our own behavior, we taught our young team how to stay positive, calm, and focused when it seemed everything around us was crumbling. Some ways were specific—arriving at the office by 8:00 a.m. as opposed to 10:00 or 11:00—others were more general. As leaders, we made sure that our actions aligned with what we expected from our team.

## Who do you know whose positive actions speak volumes?

If any of us missed the mark, especially of us at the top level, demotion was on the table; and we demonstrated that with a very visible vice president who was not pulling his weight. We let everyone know that each position at Opus would be earned and retained based on merit and contribution, and there would be consequences for anyone who was not pulling his or her load of work and responsibility. It was a powerful message and gave us the results we were seeking.

### Insight—Be Grateful

The Opus experience gave me a great opportunity to learn more about myself. As my first experience with the unique challenges of a startup, I was in unfamiliar territory. With the market crash just 40 days after I started, there were clearly times that I felt stress. At the same time, I also felt a keen sense of *gratitude* for the opportunity to work with a great group of people whom I could both teach and learn from. I learned a lot about myself during this period and know, from many employees who I stay in touch with, that many of them did also. In hindsight, the simple choice to be grateful helped set a powerful tone for growth in a very challenging environment.

## Values

There was no formal set of stated values at Opus like Our Common Bond at AT&T. But the millennials at Opus weren't looking for plaques on walls to remind them what they stood for. I learned that this wonderful group regularly practiced values like compassion, honesty, respect, loyalty, forgiveness, and kindness in how they dealt with each other and me. These values pulled us together in a powerful way.

Once we figured out how best to connect, often at local bars and coffeehouses after work rather than solely in sterile conference rooms during the day, we were successful in establishing strong relationships. It was important for me to bring values into the conversation at work. It was also important to anchor our team on things that would not change. Personally, it was crucial for me to work in an environment where the importance of connection was understood and supported.

## Business Results: Growth

After much debate, we decided to proceed with our planned IPO. When Ari and I went on our road show to pitch potential investors, in spite of the crash, we were met with a wave of cautious optimism from investors. As is the norm for these presentations, we laid out precise quarter-by-quarter forecasts for revenue increases and expense reductions. The meetings went well. On April 7, 2000, we closed at $15 per share and raised $85 million in a successful initial offering, in the middle of the crash.

It was a great start, but the air was quickly let out of our tires—we were trading below $1 within six months and delisted on NASDAQ shortly thereafter. It was a tough blow to our company. Our investors, as well as our early adopter customers saw us as a bust. After peaking over 5,000 in March of 2000, the NASDAQ composite proceeded to drop by 70 percent to just over 1,500 eighteen months later. It would take 15 years to fully recover. Understandably, our employee base was shaken. Where were the positive results?

In perhaps the most amazing performance that I have been associated with during my business career, against strong headwinds from all angles, the millennial-based team of powerful Chiefs at Opus excelled. Amazingly, we delivered on every quarterly revenue and expense commitment made during the road show for five consecutive quarters during the worst period in NASDAQ's history. This was a huge win for us. Learning every day, our team worked together and worked hard. Everyone at Opus knew how to be Chief. But it was frustrating for many of our hardworking employees to understand the disconnect between our revenue growth and our stock's performance.

At that point, it was clear that the business needed a partner, and Ari did a masterful job engineering a merger with Artemis Corporation, a software company interested in our staffing platform. It helped that we had dramatically reduced expenses and had over two years of operating cash in the bank at a time when most of our similarly positioned internet competitors had gone out of business.

The employees at Opus grew to be a powerful, high-performing unit. We were united in our understanding that human capital is the most important asset in any organization or group. We were focused on optimizing the human capital market for groups and individuals. Though our timing may have been bad, our focus was ahead of our time.

There is no doubt that the wisdom and experience of our recruited senior leadership team was invaluable during this period. As identified above in the Discipline section, there was a lot to do. There is also little doubt that one of the lessons I will remember most was provided by a talented group of millennials. They reminded me of the importance and wisdom of letting go.

## The Wisdom of Letting Go

One of the most important lessons of being Chief is the wisdom of letting go. Sometimes to drive success forward, you simply have to *be* and not *do*.

As leaders, we are taught to take responsibility for everything, when the truth is, most things are outside of our control. Yet, those at the top are supposed to have all the answers. We live in a no-excuses culture where leaders are held accountable not only for the whole of what happens, but also for every element that makes up the whole. When the pressure to live up to the expectations of others is everywhere, it can be difficult to know when to let go.

It's okay to let go of the need to be right all the time. It's also okay to let go of the need to exclusively follow the directions of others, but rather to follow your own compass, as I've implied in this book. These examples, however, are just the beginning of the wisdom of letting go. The next step is to learn that sometimes the best thing to do is actually to do nothing at all.

It should be noted that the business world understands how

the law of diminishing returns works; at some point additional investments of time, money, and resources are not justified by the return. The best strategy in many cases is simply to stop and wait for additional developments.

I remember many times at the end of a long day at Opus when a number of the senior leaders would be sitting around a conference room table planning for what might happen next. Invariably, an amazing millennial member of the team (we had loads of them) would join our table and, after adding a helpful perspective to the conversation, would ask, "Is it time for a drink?"

The truth is, at times we were all a little rattled during the market crash. Many of us naturally responded with the muscle memory of baby boomers who often employ discipline to increase the probability of success. But it is also wise to know when more work and more focus is not what's needed. In those cases, we could always count on a wise group of millennials to keep the sometimes too strong work ethic of us baby boomers in check.

Real Chiefs know that the personal clarity needed to lead effectively often comes from acceptance and stillness. I'd benefited from this understanding when I stopped chasing a mirage at AT&T, but I needed to be reminded at Opus about the true wisdom of letting go.

Letting go requires insight. The famous Serenity Prayer offers, "Grant me the serenity to accept the things I cannot change, the courage to change the things I can, and the wisdom to know the difference." Every Chief is unique, and it requires personal insight for each of us to determine what we can and cannot accept. In a culture that is often focused exclusively on results and definitions of success made by others, it takes insight to recognize when to pursue them and when to choose to let go. Only you can define what success is to you, but I speak from experience when I say that it feels much better to know that you have based your decisions and actions on what you believe is right.

There are always so many variables that we cannot directly impact. The truth is, we can envision, strategize, plan, implement, measure, make adjustments, model, enable, encourage, inspire, and question, but we cannot actually control. This is an important lesson to grasp.

If the idea of "letting it go" feels abstract to you, you might need a tool to help make it more actionable. Many organizations use the acronym RAIN (Recognition, Acceptance, Investigation, and Non-identification) to define a process that can help people thoughtfully choose their response, or lack thereof, to situations. I first became aware of RAIN while reading *The Wise Heart* by Jack Kornfield.

Recognition can be defined as awareness or consciousness. With it comes an appreciation of our choice to explore what is really happening in the moment. With exploration comes better understanding and an ability to move away from delusion.

Acceptance implies the removal of emotion and judgment from a situation to see it clearly for what it is. This can be challenging for leaders who are trained to evaluate, measure, judge, and react. Learning acceptance requires practice and discipline.

Investigation includes the search inside yourself to identify how your body reacts, how your feelings are affected, and what thoughts or images you hold as you experience the current situation.

Finally, non-identification means that you do not confuse your experience with who you truly are. A trick to help you keep a healthy perspective between the real you and what is happening to you is to see your life as a movie with you as the star. Choose to see yourself in the movie theatre watching your show. Non-identification occurs when you realize that the real you is watching the movie.

The freedom you create with RAIN can support your choice to do nothing. It is a skill that you need to develop with discipline and practice. The wisdom of letting go is an important part of being a powerful Chief. I am grateful to the millennial team at Opus for the reminder.

**Your Turn.** Please take some time to consider your own choices and their impact in building a team of Chiefs, using the following questions:

- How do you develop the insight to be grateful? What effect does it have on you?
- When are you aware of the link between your thinking and the power of your creativity?
- How do you use discipline to envision?
- When do you use support by modeling?
- How have you seen these elements lead to group success? In what other ways could they be useful to drive personal growth?
- Next, please reflect on your own ability and willingness to let go.
- In what situations are you able to let go? How do you do it? What are the results?
- When is it difficult to let go? How does that affect you? What can you do differently?

# Steering Through a Deathwatch

I had made my true media debut: headlines all across the nation were printing my name and wondering, "Is this guy insane?" It wasn't the coming-out party I had hoped for in my new role within what had been a $33 billion organization just a year earlier. Everyone was questioning whether we would make payroll and wondering who in their right mind would willingly walk on to a sinking ship.

**Background.** My New Year's resolution for 2001 was to reach out to my network of professionals and friends to plan for life after Opus 360. I was looking for an opportunity to leverage my technology background and turnaround skillsets as part of a senior team at a company where values were important. Among others I called Pat Russo, a colleague at AT&T, who had spent time at Lucent Technologies before leaving to become President at Kodak. During our discussion, I asked Pat if she thought I would be a good fit at Lucent. She said I would be a glove fit and offered to call her former employer on my behalf. Shortly after I left Opus 360 in July of 2001, I had my first interview at Lucent. Six months later, Lucent announced they had hired a new CEO—Pat Russo. Shortly thereafter I joined Lucent as Pat's first hire. At the time, Lucent was the most widely held stock in the world. It was also the poster child for the plummeting valuation of companies that had bet big on high-tech startup success. Lucent enjoyed a very large media following. Six months after I arrived, *Sales & Marketing Management* magazine put Pat on its cover with the caption, "Tough Sell: Think you've got it bad? Try selling for a struggling company like Lucent."

Thankfully, the corresponding article provided an accurate picture of the turnaround strategy we had developed and offered it as a standard for others to follow. Months later, Selling Power magazine did a similar feature article titled "How Lucent Fights Back." Here is how the article started:

> *His friends thought he was crazy. But then, what are friends for but to tell you you're nuts for taking on the impossible? And that's what it looked like when Rick Miller went after the top sales job at Lucent Technologies, a company with a once-golden reputation that had tarnished to a dull brown by the time Miller arrived on the scene. When Miller took the job of senior vice president Global Sales at Lucent Technologies last May, the once high-flying telecom's stock, which had fetched $57 in December 1999, had crashed to under $4 a share. By September 2002 it would dip below a buck a share. Everywhere there was a deathwatch, as reporters, analysts, and telecom insiders united in whispering that the once glorious company (a 1996 spin-off from AT&T) was not long for this world.*

In 2000 Lucent reported sales of $33.6 billion. At the end of 2001 sales had plummeted to $21.3 billion. When I arrived in the middle of 2002, revenue forecasts continued to fall, but the truth was no one had any idea how to forecast what lay ahead because the market was soft and the forecasting system was broken. According to Selling Power magazine, the sales force was "shattered." I would say they were powerless. Call it unwavering optimism or call it density, but I never once asked myself if I was crazy.

Actually, Selling Power missed a very important part of the story. While it is true that I was held personally accountable for increasing sales at Lucent, it is also true that none of the sales force or sales leadership actually worked for me.

Lucent Technologies relied on two product units: the fast-growing Mobility unit and the shrinking Wireline unit, which were run by two separate unit leaders. It was a change instituted by Pat's predecessor shortly before she transitioned into the role. Pat did not want the disruption of another reorganization, so she maintained the separation as is.

My job was to manage and direct two sales organizations that did not report to me. From the start, it was another challenging assignment. While I was able to employ many of the same leadership strategies I used at AT&T, role clarity was a constant issue. Nonetheless, as always, the challenge was to build a team of powerful Chiefs.

> *Your challenge, no matter the situation or organization, is to build a team of Chiefs.*

To keep sales expenses low, I leveraged Mobility and Wireline meetings to piggyback meetings with the sales leaders. I set up a Unified Sales Leadership Team (USLT) comprised of twelve regional sales vice presidents who directly reported to the two units. I traveled to meet with each leader in their region. We set up regular conference calls to create a sales rhythm. From our first meeting, most sales leaders used the USLT—and our strictly sales and sales-support focus—to recommend improvements and changes to help their people in the field.

We moved quickly to address some long-standing roadblocks. I also used a phrase that had worked well at AT&T, "Everyone at Lucent has one of two jobs, you either directly support a customer or you support somebody who does." The phrase was intended as a rallying cry for a group of separate sales forces that needed support. We needed to minimize the effect of the deathwatch talk all around us and build our own story. But talk alone is cheap—we applied our rally cry using the Compass.

### Discipline—Implement and Measure

At Lucent, the very first thing we needed to focus on was *implementation and measurement.* One of the first places we applied this discipline was sales forecasting.

Lucent had lost so much credibility in part due to their inability to accurately forecast. As I looked into the issue, I determined that the fundamental problem was one of discipline and language. At some point, virtually all salespeople are asked to forecast future sales—generally the least favorite part of a salesperson's job.

During the period of declining results, Lucent put such a large focus on forecasting that all the salespeople knew they would be reprimanded if they forecasted too high; so they responded by forecasting too low. Given senior management pressure on mid- and higher-level sales leaders to match forecasts to predetermined plans, these managers developed a system of adding positive realism to the bottom-up sales forecasts. As a result, they continued to be inaccurate and useless. As Chief, I determined, "We need both integrity in the process and a different way to forecast."

Like any change initiative, we started with training—and lots of it. Training included online tutorials, conference call training, and face-to-face in-region sessions. After training, we set a worldwide cut-over date, in which everyone had to transition away from the old probability-based forecast to one that focused on the value of potential sales at specific stages of the sales cycle—from identified to contracted. It was a hard deadline. No excuses.

We modeled the conversation at the top of the organization when we held biweekly calls with the regional sales leaders. As with every change initiative, a third of our sales professionals quickly adopted our new approach, a third took a little extra time, and a third took quite a while.

> *Consider what your group currently measures. Do you use leading and lagging indicators? Is there integrity in your measurement process?*

After three months, we added formal metrics around forecasting accuracy and used both "carrots and sticks": those who delivered sales within five percent of their forecast were regularly recognized; and those who missed were also recognized, but in a different way. At the end of six months, worldwide forecast accuracy met the five percent variance target.

Metrics and measurements beyond sales forecasting are an important part of sales leadership and reestablishing sales credibility inside any company. The discipline to use metrics as leading indicators (i.e., measuring proposals outstanding) as opposed to solely evaluating lagging indicators (i.e., revenue) proved an important part of effective leadership and being Chief.

## Support—Enable

In this specific situation, particular attention was needed in the area of enabling. As with all support elements, the key is to listen and clarify to make sure you understand what an individual or group needs. In this case it was clear. Our first priorities were to enable our team through training, compensation, recognition, and communication.

With a name like *Lucent Technologies*, unfortunately a number of people in the company believed our products sold themselves. With that assumption, we faced some push back when we set out to reinvest in our sales force.

## *Are you doing all you can to enable your team's success?*

First, we needed to convince senior management to triple the training budget. Yes, triple. Thankfully, we had an outstanding training unit that understood exactly what was needed in the field. The team had built a reputation for making every dollar count.

Part of the sales training budget established regional sales forums that brought everyone in a region together at the start of the year to not only train, but to improve team work and communication. It was also another opportunity for viral engagement to grow.

Next, we needed to increase our sales people's earnings to match their peer group in each of our geographic markets so our top performers would stay. We conducted a study to determine appropriate target compensation as well as the right mix for fixed base pay and variable commission/bonus. We then sold the concept internally for increased funding.

Third, we reestablished a two-tier recognition system in which all individuals who reached their objectives qualified for Achiever's Club; the top two percent of all sales performers qualified for Leader's Council and a four-day recognition trip that included spouses or significant others.

Finally, we supported the product houses in their efforts to increase communication with the field sales force.

Together, these strategies enabled our team to rebuild as a strong sales force.

### Mary, Jacquie, and Support

Walking into a shattered workforce, it was clear to me that employee retention was a top priority. The sales force felt abandoned by the rest of the company. I learned that a notable exception was a small team of employees responsible for sales force education. A fierce level of loyalty had been created inside that team through the leadership of their Chief, Mary Slaughter. One of her team members, Jacquie Martini, played her own role in enabling the viral growth of Mary's team of Chiefs.

Teams that reach high levels of performance do so for a reason. The team's individuals are good at what they do, and together they reach high levels of success. If you watch an NBA All-Star game, you will see the best of the best on the court succeeding together at their individual objectives. These are high scoring games featuring one spectacular basket after another. The substance of a successful team involves everyone working together on all aspects of engagement with a Chief who can combine the qualities of each such that the collective best can be expressed as a team.

Mary provided an exceptional level of support to her team and to the sales force she served. I decided to triple the sales education budget. Armed with adequate resources, Mary and her team played a major role in rebuilding the mojo of our sales force.

Mary Slaughter has that ability to support individuals in a way that makes the most of their contributions as well as their personal and professional aspirations. She combines the strengths and talents of each individual to create a great team. She is not a leader who demands unquestioned responses to her direction but welcomes, and expects, dialogue and discussion for problem-solving any situation. She recognizes that her team is filled with Chiefs who have valuable experience, perspective, and input; and she encourages everyone to have a voice, even if— especially if—it differs from her own. That experience became obvious during Mary's team's very first global sales forum.

Our company had recently renewed its investment in our sales force, and Mary was a huge part of the decision to bring the sales organization together for a three-day face-to-face event to launch the performance year with sales skills and knowledge that would help us meet the changing demands of our customers. These events were very high profile, keynoted by the CEO of the company, and with presentations from the leaders of the product and marketing groups.

At one of these events held in a large European hotel, Mary's team learned one of its first lessons: that the boss's idea might not be the best idea. After a long day of coordinating logistics for 2000 sales people, instructors, executives, and staff, it came to Jacquie's attention that one of the keynote speakers was not available for the event.

Mary debated with the Jacquie and the team about how it could be possible that one of the most anticipated speakers of the event not only was not confirmed for the engagement but also was not even in the country! Mary left the room with a clear directive: "Fix this problem, even if it means informing the audience of the program change by printing a flyer and putting it under everyone's door." So without question, Jacquie rallied the team to acquire access to expensive resources to create and print flyers, and they then proceeded to spend half of the night slipping notices under all 2000 guest room doors. The next morning everyone was fully aware that there had been a change to the schedule and understood what new content options were available to them. Jacquie and the team were exhausted but ready to accept the praise that came with a job well done.

It never came.

Later that evening, in a command center away from the hub of forum activity, Mary sat Jacquie down. She asked only one question: "What made it such a good idea for us to incur the premium expense of hotel copying services and then spend half the night hand carrying messages to everyone's hotel room?"

Jacquie was quick to respond, "Well you did, Mary."

"And why did you listen to me? It wasn't a good idea."

As the leader of this team, Mary knew very well what the end result should be, but she was not always the best person to determine the way in which the problem should be resolved. Jacquie was the expert, the one most familiar with the management of the event and responsible for managing the budget. It was her responsibility as the team's leader to look at the problem and address it meaningfully. But when Mary said,

"Fix the problem," Jacquie heard "2000 flyers."

"You are great at what you do," Mary continued, demonstrating her support. "That's why you're here. You have the expertise and authority to determine what the moves for this team are. Even more than that, your opinions and ideas are really important to the success of all of us. I trust you all to fully step into your role moving forward."

What Mary really said to Jacquie was: "You are not a soldier, but a Chief in training. You, your voice, and your opinion matter." Jacquie knew she had to act accordingly. That experience, forever known as the "flyer under the door," became Jacquie's touchstone for not blindly following a Chief. The support that Mary gave her that day was on a grand scale. She enabled Jacquie to be Chief in her own right. She taught Jacquie that power is not passed down from above. It comes from within us. We create our own power.

Very few people would argue that supporting other people isn't essential to leadership. As the training team's mission was to support others, it was even more important that they received a high level of support in kind. Mary understood that, and as Jacquie stepped into her role as Chief, she came to understand that, too. What resulted from that thriving sales support system was a thriving customer support system. Through ample support came success.

Mary taught Jacquie through that experience that there is always time to think through a resolution, to ask questions, and to rely on her own expertise. She would ask questions that made Jacquie and the rest of the team think beyond a specific task and, through self-discovery, they would realize the course of action that needed to be taken. Mary's strength is in her ability to bring out the Chief in others. Jacquie has been a powerful Chief ever since.

## Insight—Be Still

My position at Lucent was the most visible of any job in my career. National media covered my hiring. As the most widely held stock in the world, seemingly everyone had a retirement plan impacted by Lucent's poor performance. This included our customers and my neighbors. Lucent was a major employer in my home state of New Jersey and I felt the same way many Lucent employees felt when I was asked at the grocery store, at church, and at my kids' soccer games if we were going to be able to engineer a comeback.

With all the chatter going on, it was important for me to find time to *be still*. I knew I wasn't crazy, but I also knew I needed to step away from all the noise to listen to the voice inside. When I could, I'd schedule brief gaps in my normally packed schedule to slow down and simply breathe deeply for ten minutes. These short breaks allowed me to stay sharp and powerful during long days. I needed to trust my gut and I suggested to our employees that they do the same. In hindsight, the choice to be still helped a lot of us learn more about ourselves and stay strong in the midst of many distractions. Being still in today's fast-paced, multi-faceted world is more important than ever. Every Chief can take a few minutes to turn inward and tap into his or her own insight.

## Values

As an offspring of AT&T, Lucent had its own version of Our Common Bond. Lucent values included customer focus, business excellence, respect, and social responsibility. As with

AT&T, Lucent had a wide variance in the amount of conversation about these values in day-to-day operations.

I displayed these values very visibly with the USLT and in conversations with the field sales force around the world. We regularly referenced them during conference calls and meetings. Feedback from this approach was universally positive. It helped anchor our team by reinforcing the set of values employees believed was one of the important things Lucent stood for, and it was consistent across Mobility, Wireline, and all other parts of Lucent. Overall, the sales organization rallied around a focus on earning client loyalty by providing great service. Personally, it was important for me to work in an organization that focused on service as a central value.

## Business Results: No Growth?

Although we were not able to reverse a steep revenue decline, caused in large part by a market shift away from Wireline technology, we achieved a number of important milestones. First, in spite of finishing at $12.3 billion and $8.5 billion for 2002 and 2003 respectively, we returned to profitability and set the stage for growth in 2004. We also ended the deathwatch.

Second, we changed the perception of the sales force inside and outside Lucent. Publications, like *Selling Power* magazine, detailed Lucent's sales turnaround strategies as a model for others to follow. Amazing to some, Lucent was recognized— for the first and second time in consecutive years—by *Sales & Marketing Management* magazine for inclusion in its annual list of best sales forces.

Third, we changed the culture inside the sales force. In a relatively short period, we built a team of powerful Chiefs from a once shattered group of professionals and built a culture where employees felt enabled to perform. This new confidence was reflected in improving employee satisfaction survey results and also directly led to increases in customer satisfaction scores that rose to record levels.

Leading without clear positional power is the essence of being Chief. The complexities of accountability for worldwide sales performance when the sales force did not work for me provided a doctoral level course in this area. I certainly did learn about making choices when you're not in charge.

## Choices When You're Not in Charge

Being Chief is not about level or title, or even necessarily about business—instead, it's about choices. And choices are at the core of using the Power Compass to Be Chief. In many ways, the acknowledgment and understanding of our ability to choose is at the heart of our ability to succeed. Many researchers have explored the nature of how we make choices.

Two of my favorite books have tackled this important subject, and I recommend both: *The Social Animal* by David Brooks and *Thinking, Fast and Slow* by Daniel Kahneman. In particular, Kahneman's work sheds important light on the two systems that drive the way we think and make choices. The first system is fast, intuitive, and emotional. The second is slower, more deliberate, and logical. The central premise of Kahneman's work is that if you understand how you make choices, you are more likely to make better choices.

Kahneman goes on to offer six factors found to affect the quality of choice making—specifically, increased experience, patience, persistence, and humility—along with an understanding of natural human bias and diversity of input all improve the quality of decision making.

But here's the simple truth about choices when you're not in charge: we live and work in a world with people of many different levels and titles, and where everyone has a boss. From the entry-level trainee, who seemingly reports to everyone, all the way up to the CEO (who reports to the board), everyone answers to someone. We don't always have the ability to unilaterally choose what we want in the workplace. Yet, we always have the opportunity to be powerful.

At Lucent, regional sales leaders reported to product unit Chiefs, yet I was accountable to the CEO for overall sales performance. What did I do? I used the following list to maximize my impact:

- Envision broadly – See the opportunity from beyond just your part of the organization.
- Plan inclusively – Incorporate support groups in any strategy session.
- Measure outside the lines – Keep track of support-group key measures and performance.
- Shamelessly adopt – Find the best practices from peer groups. Adopt them, and recognize the originators.
- Communicate consistently and consciously – Use words to connect, and be sure the words you think, write, and speak are aligned with your actions.
- Own it – See yourself as Chief with responsibility across organization lines.
- Live it – Make your values visible, in particular with regard to teamwork.
- Assume the position – Always put yourself in your boss's

seat before you bring an issue or decision "up." Bring the person in charge multiple options with pros and cons before you offer your recommendation.

- Be empathic – Remember that you may be working for someone who is also not in charge, in that his or her word is not final. Have some empathy for your boss, too.

You do not have to be "on top" to put the Power Compass to good use. By recognizing and developing the qualities that bring out the Chief in others, you can achieve success at any endeavor, large or small. The choice, as always, is up to you. It helps when you realize that you are always in charge of what matters.

**Your Turn.** Please take some time to consider your own choices and their impact on building a team of Chiefs, using the following questions:

- Have you developed the insight to be still? If so, what effect does it have on you?
- In what ways do you use your spoken words to increase the power of your creativity?
- How do you use discipline to implement and measure?
- How do you use support to enable?
- How have these elements lead to group success? In what other ways could they be used to drive personal growth?

Next, reflect on choices you make when you're not in charge:

- In what areas are you most experienced? How do the choices you make in these areas differ with the choices you make in areas in which you are not as experienced?
- What biases do you have that have helped determine

the choices you make? What biases hinder your choices?

- When in your personal and professional life does patience and persistence pay off?
- How does humility play a role in the choices you make?
- When do you seek diverse opinions as a strategy for decision-making? How does it help you broaden your perspective?

# Serving a Team of Warfighters

To my surprise, a new employee arrived to consolidate management of the sales forces. It became clear that Lucent did not need me to run sales staff operations only. During that time, I often felt powerless. After several weeks of transition, he suggested I look for another position inside the company or consider leaving. This was a tough time for Lucent and for me. Lucent was looking for growth opportunities and so was I. Lucent's biggest growth opportunity came from a market that the company had abandoned several years earlier. I volunteered for yet another turnaround, but this one would take me to places I never could have imagined. And I regained my power.

**Background.** Lucent had been limiting its sales focus exclusively to telecommunications suppliers; they were aware that a move back into the corporate market might set up unwanted competition with some of its largest customers. At the same time, the company had been studying reentry into the U.S. federal market, a market the company had (for the most part) withdrawn from years earlier. Lucent hired Dr. Phil Anderson, a former Marine, to do a reentry feasibility study. I had been gutted by the news I was going to be replaced, but now felt drawn to the challenge Lucent was undertaking. With years of government experience during my years with Unisys, I approached Pat Russo and said, "Pat, I think I can help you lead the rebuilding of the government business." Pat agreed and, luckily, Phil decided to join the team. I knew we would not get any added investment dollars until we proved we could stop the revenue decline in the unit. The key for the newly established

Lucent Government Solutions unit would be to rebuild and reestablish the confidence of current and prospective customers in the government market. My personal goal was to reestablish the federal government as a key growth driver within Lucent. As always, the key to both was to build a team of Chiefs in Government Solutions. First, we needed to rebuild trust, and that came with some big challenges. "The trust problem is big," Phil said as we were discussing our plan moving forward. "But I completely understand why it's lacking." The government unit, or what remained of it, had lost 25 percent of its revenue over the prior two years. Long-term customers were angry and vocal. They were not pleased with Lucent's decision to close the Washington D.C. office and pull back from government business. Many of our existing customers remained simply because they did not have the budget necessary to leave Lucent and convert to another vendor. With our very visible departure from Washington, they were also aware Lucent had stopped developing government market-specific features for their hardware. Although the sales force maintained an "I'm on your side" perspective, the customer base could be summarized in one word: upset.

I learned that reentering a market is a lot more difficult than opening a new market. It takes a lot of work to get back to even, particularly when the customer base is convinced you have hung them out to dry. This was a close-knit government market in which everyone seemed to talk to everyone else, effectively eliminating any chance of new account marketing until our base was satisfied.

Despite these impediments, Phil and I were enthusiastic when we joined the team. This group of professionals impressed both of us with their knowledge of the market and the strong relationships they had maintained with customers over the years. With under $200 million in declining revenue and a market that had little in common with the rest of Lucent's customers—a base that generated more than $8 billion in revenue—this great group of people were accustomed to little attention and support. We looked forward to changing that.

When we arrived and announced our intention to build a billion dollar government business, the palpable skepticism was understandable. By eliminating any presence in Washington years earlier, we were all but invisible to anyone other than our existing customers. At the time, our largest customer group was limited to several army bases that utilized a dated contracting vehicle. These customers were loyal yet even they were cynical about our future plans.

We also needed to quickly show Lucent senior management that we could turn the situation around, grow organically, and earn their confidence. It was understood that we would identify key acquisitions and build a new billion dollar business, providing the company much needed growth and market diversification. Here's how we applied the Power Compass.

## Discipline—Strategize

At Government Solutions, the very first thing we needed to do was *strategize* and develop a market plan to rebuild trust and create a targeted customer plan to focus our limited resources in order to grow.

*Consider the definition of strategy as deciding what you are not going to do. Does your group have the discipline to say no?*

Over the past two years, the unit had simply focused on retaining as many customers as possible. We decided to shift to longer-term, strategic thinking focused on growth by rebuilding our presence and regaining market visibility. We did this by figuring out what we were not going to do. It is important to get input from diverse groups of knowledgeable people when setting a strategy. We consulted with a variety of sources for a broad range of internal and external points of view on where we needed to refocus for sustainable growth.

We decided we could not pursue new business aggressively in the civilian segment. Given the size and complexity of the federal government market, with limited resources we determined the best strategy was to focus our efforts on the Department of Defense (DOD) in general and specifically on the unique communications needs of our nation's warfighters. Four key decisions oriented around that target proved to have a positive impact.

First, we had to re-establish a presence in Washington D.C. We rented office space and reopened a Government Affairs Office. Second, we decided to showcase the capabilities of our Bell Labs unit and built a Bell Labs Network Reliability and Security Center, collocated with the Government Affairs Office. Third, we established a government partner program to extend the reach of our limited direct sales force. Fourth, under Phil's guidance we established a government advisory board of well-known leaders who were interested in helping us to leverage Bell Labs' resources to support our troops.

It took discipline to adhere to our narrowed focus and forsake the potential of new business in the civilian sphere but we regained a lot of credibility with both our clients and our employees with this clearly communicated strategy.

### Support—Inspire

When I arrived, I found a sales and sales support group that was incredibly resilient. They were indeed a powerful unit. Many of them had served this market for decades and had seen (and outlasted) plenty of inexperienced managers who had come in and promised change. They had learned to be skeptical because these promises were generally followed by a downsizing as new managers, who did not understand the long government sales cycle, could not get "corporate" to set appropriate and reasonable plans. Prior managers also chose to focus on short-term profitability rather than revenue growth. *Inspiration* would be a tough sell to this group of skeptics.

To further complicate the situation, the government workforce was split between a small group of sales professionals in the Washington suburbs and a larger service delivery and support organization in Greensboro, North Carolina. I learned quickly that the Greensboro team was fearful that new management would attempt to consolidate the government team and relocate them to the greater Washington area. Unlike their partners in Washington, who did not at first feel "safe to say," this seasoned team had no issue with voicing their opinions. I was closing my first all-hands meeting with the Greensboro team: "Can I answer some questions?" A well-dressed woman in the second row politely raised her hand. She stood up, looked me dead in the eye and asked, "Why should we believe you?"

## *Consider people who inspire you. What can you learn from these individuals?*

I had a lot of work to do to get back to zero with this group of employees before we could make any real progress. I also knew that there was very little I could say to win them over—I had to show them that I deserved their trust. In that first meeting, I borrowed from the same playbook I always used. I was firm on generalities and vague on specifics. I spoke a lot about Lucent's values and told them I asked for this job, I was not recruited into it. Still, her blunt question had taken me aback. I answered as best I could, following up with, "And I do not expect you to believe me until I return for the tenth time." They laughed, but I saw a lot of heads nod, which was encouraging.

Over the next several months, I returned regularly to Greensboro. The Greensboro team taught me about our government base of customers, and I may have surprised them by actually listening. Together, we worked to fix the company's damaged reputation and celebrated small victories. They learned to trust that I would do what I said I would. They also saw me spend a lot of my time with their customers. Relationships were built over time and respect was earned the same way.

When the unit's fear of relocation slowly faded and smiles appeared when corporate earnings reports started including success in the government market, many of the skeptics turned into allies. When I openly shared my concerns about whether headquarters would continue support for our market when corporate results continued to languish, I had become one of the team. While it is true that I may have inspired some of them, they clearly inspired me. Inspiring others also means being inspired yourself.

## Insight—Be Generous

The Government Solutions experience gave me an opportunity to work with a caring employee group. At our Washington D.C., Tysons Corner, Virginia, and Greensboro, North Carolina locations, our employees extended *generosity* into their communities, supporting many nonprofit activities. As we worked together to rebuild Lucent's government business, this generosity was also visible in the way we treated each other. It was important for me personally to work in this type of environment and it helped me learn more about myself.

In hindsight, the choice to be generous also helped set the tone for growth in a very challenging environment. Once again, it was an intersection of my personal values and my professional values and it was perfectly aligned with the members of my team. Engaging in something that demonstrated our personal value systems fostered our mutual respect. We were acknowledging each other as Chiefs.

## Values

Government employees at Lucent shared the same understanding of the corporate values statements as their nongovernment peers. In my experience, however, our government employees took those values statements to heart like few others. In addition, these employees held themselves accountable to what they believed was an equally important set of values set by their market.

With customers who included all types, ranging from administrators to warfighters, our employees adopted their values of public service, duty, honor, country, and sacrifice. As a team, we built strong relationships with our customers. As I demonstrated to our employees that I understood, agreed with, vocally supported, and lived the values that our market expected, I was able to build lasting relationships with both employees and customers. It was an honor to work with both groups.

## Phil, Kathy, and Values

As a values-based organization, the government unit was packed with people who fit my i3K ideal. I had generally been drawn to people who display intelligence, intensity, integrity, and kindness, and specifically to those who wear their values proudly on their sleeves. This description uniformly describes the amazing employees in our unit. And Phil Anderson is a great example of such a Chief.

As a true servant leader, Phil led with humility, tenacity, honesty, respect, empathy, and commitment. In reconstituting a Washington office for our government unit, Phil pulled together a strong group of people, who then became powerful Chiefs themselves. One in particular, Kathy Cowles, did an amazing job leading the marketing efforts that reintroduced Lucent to a market we had abandoned years earlier. It is clear that Phil influenced Kathy, but there is also no doubt that Kathy played her own role enabling the viral growth of Chiefs. Not surprisingly, these two got started on the right foot.

In 2003 Kathy received a random phone call. Phil was on the

other end of the line: "Hey Kathy. I'm wondering whether you would be interested in a senior marketing manager position on my new government relations and strategy team with Lucent Technologies?" Kathy was jazzed and immediately wanted the job. As she prepped for the interview, she wondered what Phil might be looking for, what strengths she could bring, what role she could play, and who else he might be considering for the role. As she drove to the interview, however, Kathy made a decision: "No selling, no hype—I am just going to be myself."

The two clicked immediately. Kathy listened to his vision, Phil was interested in her skills and background, and they talked about family and had a laugh or two. Kathy was soon offered the position and moved into our new offices on N.Y. Avenue in Washington D.C.

Phil commanded leadership. He was disciplined and fair, but firm. Frankly, he had a tough job. In spite of being a military outsider and not "one of the ole' Lucent boys," he was in every way possible the leader he needed to be. To be honest, building a team as an outside hire and creating those trusts and values to quickly build each other up for the common goal is no easy task.

For Kathy, leadership started with the feeling that you are respected and valued, that the person you work for is respected and valued, and so on, up the chain. The alignment was clear. Phil was a powerful leader, and he inspired others to be powerful too. Show up, be prepared, do your job, and along the way make sure you take care of each other. Kathy and Phil's adherence to these values is what kept the team cohesive in demanding times.

We had a lot going on at that time. It was a time of great opportunity for growth, but it was also a time of great challenge. The government is very diverse, with unique communications needs, buying characteristics, acquisition methods, funding cycles, and of course, political will. And, as our team was growing, we saw the challenges through a multitude of market and technical lenses. There was the complex armed forces transformation, public safety and critical infrastructure protection, the beginnings of e-government, new paradigms in network security important to our Bell Labs work, and of course, Iraq and the large and complex reconstruction projects. Everyone on the team had a view, a priority, and a need for funding. I was glad to have Chiefs like Phil and Kathy in the unit.

The first thing Phil wanted to do was to develop the vision, mission, strategy, and tactics—he was in his element. As a Marine, having and executing against a plan is innate. It is about constant dialogue and making each person feel a commitment to the mission of the team. He and Kathy led a diverse group with unique personalities and backgrounds, and Phil knew how to get the best out of them. He wanted each person to have a part in creating the strategic plan—he wanted them all to be powerful Chiefs. Kathy's role was to ensure they had a unified, clear, and direct marketing plan that would benefit the entire government team and help that team reach their sales commitment to the corporation.

One of their key focuses was on public safety, and the team worked diligently on the issue. Phil and his leaders were focused and determined to make a difference there. This was three years after the disaster and heroism of 9/11, and our first responders, health professionals, and military forces still struggled to share critical information. At the time, public safety communications were based primarily on older voice technology and were not well suited to responding to a new terrorist threat and the associated complex data-driven requirements of the 21st century.

Under Phil's leadership and his constant focus, his team was dedicated to changing that. The 9/11 Commission Report bluntly stated the need to address the most pressing problems associated with the nation's ability to respond to the next inevitable attack. The Commission tersely stated it: "The inability to communicate was a critical element at the World Trade Center, the Pentagon, and Somerset County, Pennsylvania crash sites, where multiple agencies and multiple jurisdictions responded."

At Lucent, we knew that the technology existed to provide critical data, voice, and multimedia connectivity to enable public safety professionals to respond to crises and save American lives.

Phil and Kathy fully believed that deploying a solution that utilized the most advanced technologies available in the commercial wireless market would also provide huge cost savings to the United States. We felt that this system could be deployed in key regions within six months, and would create a dedicated national public safety communications capability within 24 months.

It was clear that what united and drove Phil's team, and the rest of the Government unit, was a total commitment to the values of duty, honor, sacrifice, and service to our country.

Ten years later, it is something Phil and Kathy are still actively working for, albeit with different organizations. Phil had influence not just on Kathy, but on the entire organization. It was the simplicity of his value system that proved to be the most impactful influence on Kathy's career and leadership style. Four specific values come to mind:

- Purpose produces passion and energizes like nothing else;
- Treat everyone the way you would like to be treated;
- Make a difference every day to someone or something (or both); and
- Have a good laugh—it is magic for the soul!

Four values, embodying all qualities of being Chief.

## Business Results: Growth

It is amazing what happens when you properly support people who are already a team of powerful Chiefs. The team was able to quickly deliver impressive results once they trusted the direction we were taking and trusted me as Chief. Against the backdrop of a 25 percent revenue loss over the prior 24 months, we reversed trajectory, grew revenue by 30 percent during the first year, and received Lucent's top business unit award. The key was rebuilding trust and reestablishing confidence with both current and prospective customers, and we did that by rebuilding trust and reestablishing confidence within our ranks. It was viral engagement in action. Our employees felt inspired to be Chiefs themselves and to merge who they were with the work they were doing. The shift was palpable.

In our second year, we repeated as award winners with another 30 percent growth year. Our success was recognized when Lucent received its first market share growth award from the Frost and Sullivan organization for our performance in the government sector. Lucent rose to #44 on Input's ranking of the top 150 federal contractors. Customer and employee satisfaction survey results hit all-time highs. As we grew our workforce, employees outside the government group wanted to join us. Our team of Chiefs designed and developed a strong government ethics program to reinforce best practices and teach newcomers what was expected in the government market.

During this period we also had a signature win. To the surprise of many, we were awarded a contract to provide the DOD with up to $1 billion in communication services in support of their mission in Iraq.

While total revenue to Lucent from actual purchase orders issued against the blanket contract vehicle amounted to under $200 million over two years, the award signaled to the entire market that Lucent Government Solutions had quickly become a major force in the market. Actual purchase orders were primarily focused on building a wireless network to support public safety in major cities in Iraq. Notably, this capability played a major role in facilitating the first elections in Iraq. We all felt a sense of pride when the media broadly shared pictures of smiling Iraqi citizens proudly displaying their purple fingers, signifying their status as first-time voters. This contract also enabled us to record a third consecutive year of 30 percent growth.

## Engaging the Quiet Chiefs

When I took over Lucent's Government Operations, I was confident in our ability to turn around the unit in part based on many great suggestions made by a group of strong, vocal employees in Washington, DC and Greensboro, NC. By and large, these employees were visible and forceful in sharing their views of what it would take to regain customer trust. But it was also a third group of employees located in Whippany, NJ, who quietly played a big role in our comeback. This team worked for

Bell Labs.

Today, people marvel at the innovation coming out of Silicon Valley from firms like Google and Apple, companies that top the most admired lists. Not long ago, the hallmark for innovation resided on the opposite coast, in Murray Hill, NJ, at the headquarters of Bell Laboratories. Born out of the original American Telephone & Telegraph (AT&T) company in 1925, researchers working at Bell Labs are credited with the development of the transistor, the laser, the UNIX operating system, and information theory itself. Eight Nobel Prizes have been awarded for work completed at Bell Labs.

The good news for me was Bell Labs had a long history, and a dedicated unit, focused on providing advanced technology to the U.S. government.

Walking into my new assignment, I had clear ideas about how to increase the productivity of my sales force. Having "grown up" in a sales environment I was accustomed to working with a gregarious peer group of people who made a living by talking. For example, I was an early adopter of an "open office" approach years earlier at AT&T that was highlighted in the Harvard Business Review. Creating space that increased conversations was one of the goals. It worked well.

But the first time I walked into Bell Labs, I knew I was in a different space. This was a place optimized for introverts.

I immediately noticed the large number of small offices lined up off the main corridors. And I noticed the silence. I learned about the many different ways Bell Labs employees created and reinforced viral engagement, helping these brilliant thinkers bring out their very best. I saw that big team meetings were few and far between and that email was often the preferred communication tool, even between colleagues in adjoining offices. Many chose to enjoy lunch breaks without leaving their offices, or when the weather permitted, by taking walks around the building grounds, alone. Perhaps my biggest lesson was that viral engagement among introverts is more subtle, but just as impactful, as viral engagement among extroverts.

## *How can you bring out the very best from the third to half of your team who are introverts?*

Here are my top takeaways:

- Lead time can create better quality.
- Small groups can enable more contribution than large groups.
- Written communication allows for thoughtful responses.
- Directed questions clearly identify expectations.
- Team building needs to be structured so it works for everyone.
- Office space can be configured to support creativity.
- Technology improves communication, via social media and on-line chat tools.
- Diversity of approach can be important.
- Individual challenges sometimes work best.
- Anonymity can be a good thing.

Chiefs at all levels in Bell Labs connected what they did to who they were, and management understood what it took to support a primarily introverted culture. These Chiefs were powerful in their own ways. And the results were amazing. Our government unit's dramatic growth was fueled by Bell Labs innovations.

Subsequent to my government assignment, I read *Quiet: The Power of Introverts in a World That Can't Stop Talking* by Susan Cain.

It is a must-read for anyone committed to engaging any team.

In addition to a deep dive into the world of introverts, Susan offers the following central insight: "[We] would be better off if we appreciated that not everyone aspires to be a leader in the conventional sense of the word—that some people wish to fit harmoniously into the group, and others to be independent of it. Often the most highly creative people are in the latter category." With introvert estimates as high as 50 percent of some groups, it's high time we all learn how to better engage the quiet Chiefs.

Sustainable growth depends on it.

**Your Turn.** Next, please take some time to consider your own choices and their impact in building a team of Chiefs, using the following questions:

- When do you develop the insight to be generous? What effect does it have on you?
- In what ways do your actions increase the power of your creativity?
- How do you use discipline to strategize?
- When do you use support to inspire?
- How have these elements led to group success? In what other ways could they be used to drive personal growth?

## Sustainable Growth

As part of the last stages of our contract in Iraq, the members of our Lucent Government team serving in Baghdad were helping the U.S. Department of Defense personnel transition support for our public safety wireless network to the Iraqi government. It had been a challenging assignment in a war zone, but for more than two years, they had served alongside our DOD partners with distinction. And more importantly, their work had directly supported the first free democratic vote in Iraq's history. Their work also brought benefits to those of us back in the States as news of Lucent's performance spread throughout the military community. We were invited to participate in bids with groups that had excluded Lucent prior to our Iraq experience. Our sales force reported a corollary benefit in the civilian community where doors that had previously been closed to us were suddenly opening as well. We were positioned for growth. Yet at the same time, and not without a twinge of bitter irony, Lucent Technologies itself was in its last stages as an independent company.

As the company's core business continued to shrink, Lucent had begun to look for a partner. Toward the end of 2006, they found one at France-based Alcatel, a communications company whose strong position in Europe would complement Lucent's strong North American position. When the companies announced the merger, the implications for our government business, and my place in the company were clear.

When the Alcatel deal was announced, I was not the only one who recognized that things were about to drastically change. Other senior Lucent Officers starting scrambling for positions within the newly merged company. It was a C-suite free-for-all, and I wanted no part of it. Combined with the likelihood of declining corporate and customer support for our growing Government unit, management and I agreed it was time for me to leave the company. I was optimistic and began to make lists of other major technology companies and executive search firms to contact. This would not be the end of the road for me. At the same time, another question was lurking: Should I even be looking for another turnaround opportunity or should I think about a completely different path?

Leaving Lucent, as I did with every transition I'd made in my 25-year career, I knew I had to once again look for opportunities to create sustainable growth. And I knew that wherever I went my focus would be on using my roadmap to build a team of powerful Chiefs.

But I also needed to figure out how I could create more flexibility in my schedule and make family time a much higher priority. I had missed a lot and my kids were entering high school. What if I could create a job working for myself? We'd saved enough money for me to try something new. The economy was strong, and opening a consulting business seemed like a good idea. Why not start my own company, in which I could help leaders build teams of Chiefs in different companies?

I founded my own business. Today it's called Being Chief LLC, and I offer my services as a confidential advisor (and confidant) to business leaders and as a speaker to a broad range of organizations. I have been able to leverage my experience with what I call the six C's: customers, competitors, costs, capital, community, and culture. I'm also able to apply the Compass I used personally over the previous 30 years more broadly across a more diverse group of clients to help them build power teams that achieve sustainable growth. It has been a rewarding experience, and it has also given me an opportunity to expand both my understanding of sustainable growth and employee engagement.

As I started my next chapter, a shift was also happening in the market. In 2006, Andrew Savitz published *The Triple Bottom Line*, using case studies to describe how the best-run companies were succeeding with a focus on their economic bottom line (profit), their social bottom line (people), and their environmental bottom line (planet).

At the same time, CEO Sam Palmisano was promoting IBM's focus on four key questions to drive sustainable growth. The first three were in line with what I had learned about employees, shareholders, and customers.

- Why would someone work for you?
- Why would someone invest his or her money with you?
- Why would someone spend their money with you— what is unique about you?
- Why would society allow you to operate in their region?

It was the last question that spoke to Savitz's treatise and which caused me to again expand my thinking on sustainable growth, in three ways.

First, it expanded my recognition of the *impact* of an organization and got me thinking about what outcomes are required to claim success within a specific community. Now, being a good corporate citizen in the community included more than making an occasional philanthropic donation for social good or caring for the environment beyond simply not polluting. Note: Sam's fourth question raised the bar and required more than a "do no immediate harm" approach; it requires a "make it better" solution.

Second, this new question also shifted my perspective about *time*. Unlike the first three questions that had an unspoken time frame of "quarter to quarter" or "year to year," this question shifted my thinking from the short term to the truly long term. Thinking in terms of "decade to decade" or "century to century," such that it could continue indefinitely also set a new bar.

Finally, I understood this last question was also linked to *employee engagement*. To unlock the power in their employees, companies now need to show all constituency groups that they are seriously committed to a long-term focus on making a positive impact on society.

As I work with clients today, we focus on steps that will produce sustainable growth for employees, customers, and investor's quarter after quarter and year after year, and where the greater community at large is enhanced or improved decade after decade and into the next millennium.

Said differently, I have always known I needed to enable a team of Chiefs to maintain sustainable growth, but today I also know that I need to focus on sustainable growth to maintain a team of Chiefs.

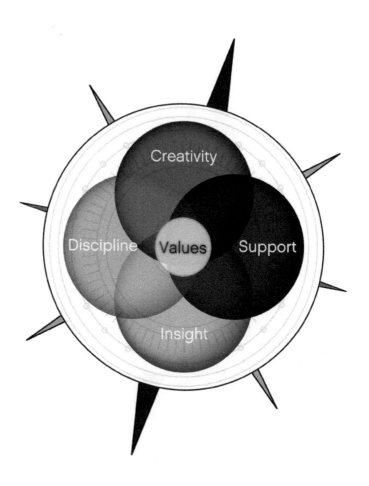

# THREE

# Your Power Compass

*For me, to be Chief is to mindfully work to be the best version of yourself. I'm no life coach, however; I'm a business leader. My company and this book are both focused on offering simple choices to help you connect what you do to who you are, determining the direction you want to go next, and unlocking your power to be Chief. The first step is for you to create your own Compass. The next step is to make sure your Compass is as powerful as you want to be. This section will help you do both, step by step.*

# Create Your Power Compass

## Step One – Set Your Core Values

As we've discussed throughout this book, your values are the foundation of your Power Compass—the cornerstones of who you are and the crucial points of alignment for what you will do as Chief. Your values guide the direction you take, and fuel your power.

Your first step, then, is to determine which of your values are most important to you.

Select your four most strongly held values and write them below. You can use the sample Values from the list on the following page or add your own.

## Sample Values

| | | | |
|---|---|---|---|
| Accountability | Empathy | Joy | Risk Taking |
| Accuracy | Empowerment | Kindness | Self Expression |
| Acknowledgement | Equality | Leadership | Sensitivity |
| Adventure | Ethics | Nurturing | Serenity |
| Authenticity | Excellence | Orderliness | Service |
| Beauty | Family | Originality | Spirituality |
| Collaboration | Free Spirit | Participation | Spontaneity |
| Community | Freedom to Choose | Partnership | Strength |
| Comradeship | Harmony | Passion | Success |
| Connection | Honesty | Performance | Tenderness |
| Courage | Humor | Personal Power | Trust |
| Creativity | Imagination | Productivity | Truth |
| Dedication | Independence | Recognition | Wealth |
| Directness | Integrity | Respect | Wisdom |

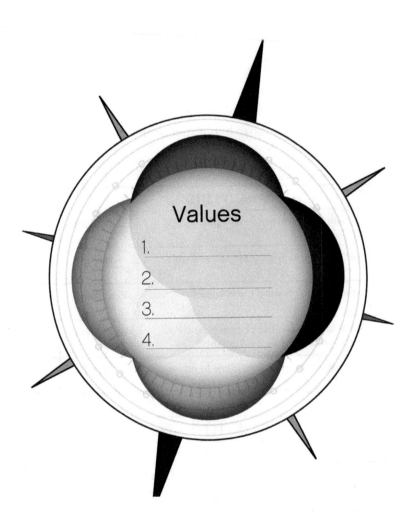

Values

1. _____

2. _____

3. _____

4. _____

## Step Two – Establish Your Power Compass Baseline

For each of the 25 questions, circle the number 0–4 that best describes you, and then total your score in each of the five categories. Once you have completed all 25 quesions add up the *TOTALS from all* five areas for your personal: POWER COMPASS BASELINE SCORE. If you'd like to build your compass online, go to beingchief.com/compass.

(0=Never, 1=Sometimes, 2=Often, 3=Consistently, 4=Always)

| DISCIPLINE | | SCORE |
|---|---|---|
| Do I describe what I do in a broad, positive context? | Envision | 0 1 2 3 4 |
| Do I build specific approaches to succeed with the help of others? | Strategize | 0 1 2 3 4 |
| Do I create and use detailed plans to reach goals? | Plan Tactics | 0 1 2 3 4 |
| Do I follow those plans, track progress, and hold myself accountable for my performance? | Implement/ Measure | 0 1 2 3 4 |
| Do I anticipate changes and welcome input from all sources? | Adjust | 0 1 2 3 4 |
| | *D-Total* | |

| CREATIVITY | | SCORE |
|---|---|---|
| Do I trust my feelings as truth and guidance? | Feel | 0 1 2 3 4 |
| Do I take responsibility for my thoughts and can I stop negative thinking when I become aware of it? | Think | 0 1 2 3 4 |
| Do I choose words consciously when I speak because words are powerful? | Speak | 0 1 2 3 4 |
| Do I write to express what I feel and what I think? | Write | 0 1 2 3 4 |
| Do I act in ways that are consistent with what I feel, think, and say? | Act | 0 1 2 3 4 |
| | *C-Total* | |

| SUPPORT | | SCORE |
|---|---|---|
| Do I ask others about their views, motives, and assumptions, and listen? | Question | 0  1  2  3  4 |
| Do I "walk the talk" to demonstrate what I believe to others? | Model | 0  1  2  3  4 |
| Do I motivate others more from who I am, rather than what I may say? | Inspire | 0  1  2  3  4 |
| Do I actively support others with what they need once I understand their needs? | Enable | 0  1  2  3  4 |
| Do I cheer for others? | Encourage | 0  1  2  3  4 |
| | *S-Total* | |

| INSIGHT | | SCORE |
|---|---|---|
| Can I quiet my mind to listen to the voice inside me? | Still | 0  1  2  3  4 |
| Do I accept people and circumstances as they are and forgive all, including myself, for past mistakes? | Accepting | 0  1  2  3  4 |
| Am I generous with my time and possessions? | Generous | 0  1  2  3  4 |
| Am I grateful for life's gifts? | Grateful | 0  1  2  3  4 |
| Do I live in the current moment? | Present | 0  1  2  3  4 |
| | *I-Total* | |

| VALUES | SCORE |
|---|---|
| Do I feel strongly about my values? | 0  1  2  3  4 |
| Do I think about the values I stand most strongly for? | 0  1  2  3  4 |
| Do I discuss the values I stand most strongly for with others? | 0  1  2  3  4 |
| Do I write about the values I stand most strongly for? | 0  1  2  3  4 |
| Do I act in ways that are consistent with my values? | 0  1  2  3  4 |
| *V-Total* | |

| MY POWER COMPASS BASELINE | *TOTAL* | |
|---|---|---|

There are no right or wrong answers in your Power Compass Baseline, and you may be happy with all of your current choices and resulting scores. But if you determine that your choices aren't getting you (or your organization) where you want to be, or as fast as you want to get there, it might be time for a change. What needs to change is up to you. That's where your Power Compass can be particularly helpful.

## Step Three – Make Your Compass More Powerful

The Power Compass offers 25 opportunities for you to make small changes that can have a big impact in:

- Clarifying what you stand for
- Deepening your self-understanding
- Increasing the probability of your success
- Strengthening your relationships
- Learning to align the ways you manifest the future

If you notice areas within your Power Compass Baseline that you would like to change, note them below. You can even refer to specific Baseline questions. They make a fantastic starting point.

*Example: Creativity/Act, I choose to act in ways that are more aligned with what I think, do, and say. Today, I do it often, but moving forward, I choose to do it consistently.*

Specific Areas of Focus:
1.
2.
3.

As you more consistently and successfully *create* your future with *discipline* and *support* for and from others, aligned with expanding *insight* as you live your values, you will become more powerful.

The 25 questions that make up the Power Compass Baseline offer a range of choices you can make to increase your power as you step into your role as Chief. Another option is to reflect back on the Your Turn questions in Parts One and Two. Where could you make a change that feels right to you? Once you decide if the change is something to which you can dedicate your efforts, write it down and commit to reassess your choices in 90 days. Being a more powerful Chief is, in fact, being more of who you are. And you can choose how powerful you want to be as Chief.

That power will also influence everyone around you and increase the chances that they will become more powerful. Like any good compass, your Power Compass will help you navigate your path. If you'd like to accelerate the pace of your team becoming more powerful, consider sharing the Power Compass Baseline process with others.

This is the power of being Chief.

# Summary

Looking back at these varied experiences, from the outskirts of Boston to the inside of the Green Zone in Baghdad, I realize now that although I have traveled on many different paths I have been guided by an important compass.

In each instance, the five parts of the Power Compass helped teams create cultures of engaged employees where people made positive choices, excelled, and everyone could be Chief. As a result, productivity, innovation, teamwork, and quality became the new norm. Completely engaged and supported Chiefs at all levels also allowed us to decentralize and increase the speed of many decisions, delivering better results for customers, shareowners, and for each other. And perhaps the best news was that any employee could inspire their peers to be Chief, too, increasing power to the rest of the group. In each case, teams of highly engaged Chiefs made all the difference.

More recently, this same Compass has helped Chiefs at all levels in companies across many industries create conditions for viral engagement and step up to a new broader definition and a longer-term view of sustainable success that includes improving conditions for members of the community at-large, in perpetuity.

At a time when so many organizations and groups are in need of stronger leadership, I urge you to consider your opportunity to build teams of Chiefs. And remember that the concept of *being* is every bit as important as the concept of being *Chief*. Look inside yourself for the direction and strength you need. Increase your insight and build your creativity. Connect your personal and professional life. Exercise discipline where it is needed and support others with insight when they need it, always with a steadfast commitment to your values.

I also ask you to thoughtfully consider the power of your values. We need leaders to make good choices in families, communities, governments, social agencies, educational institutions, and ministries, as well as in business. It really doesn't matter if you have the title of Chief or any other title. We need you to help create cultures where all leaders can excel and become more resilient.

Ask yourself the following five questions on a regular basis to help guide your choices to build teams of Chiefs and to be the best Chief you can be:

- How can living my *values* bring out the best in me and those around me?
- How can I *develop* insight to learn more about myself?
- How can I use *creativity* to increase my positive impact?
- How can I use *discipline* to manage better?
- How can I *support* others to increase their positive impact?

Although this Compass is offered as a tool to help you succeed, it is certainly not offered as the only path. I suggest you take a utilitarian view of the information provided and develop your own, perhaps unique, view of how to build a team of Chiefs and incorporate the pieces you like into your own style of leadership. I also encourage you to be wary of anyone who offers the definitive answer to anything. Similarly, be wary of anyone who provides the path to leadership. Perhaps the best advice comes from Vaclav Havel who offers, "Keep the company of those who seek the truth, and run from those who have found it." And remember, anyone can be Chief.

Whatever path you choose, look inside yourself for true power. You don't need permission or approval from anyone else, ever. And you certainly don't need a title.

As Glinda, the good witch of the north, said in *The Wizard of Oz*: "You had the power all along."

Connect what you *do* to who you *are*. Be more of who you are. Make the choice to be Chief.

# Index

## A

Act, 48
Adjust, 54, 99
Andrew Savitz
    *The Triple Bottom Line, 163*
Ari Horowitz, 115
AT&T, 72, 82, 91, 103, 158

## B

Barry Posner
    *Leadership Challenge: How to Get*
    *Extraordinary Things Done in*
    *Organizations, 57*
Be Accepting, 41, 104
Be Generous, 41, 141
Be Grateful, 42, 122
Be Present, 94
Be Still, 139
Bell Labs, 148, 158
Bentley University, 13
Bernie Ebbers, 97, 105, 108
Bob Allen, 72, 97
Brené Brown
    *The Gifts of Imperfection, 112*
    *Daring Greatly, 112*
Bumper stickers, 88

## C

Carlos Cashman, 115
Columbia University, 56
Common Bond, 75, 95, 101, 108,
    123, 139
Creativity, 43, 48, 88
Customer Value Added (CVA), 72

## D

Daniel Kahneman
    *Thinking, Fast and Slow, 141*
David Brooks
    *The Social Animal, 141*
Day-One Speeches, 74, 81
Discipline, 29, 50, 83
Disciplined Human Resource
    Management, 109

## E

Early Lessons, 80
Economic Value Added (EVA), 72
Employee engagement, 65, 95
Enable, 59
Encourage, 59, 85
Envision, 53, 118
EQ—emotional intelligence, 78

## F

Feel, 48
First Steps, 74, 98
Fortune Magazine, 72, 76

## G

Gail McGovern, 73
Go-test, 77

## I

i3k, 46, 78, 152
IBM, 36, 43, 116
Implement and measure, 54. 132
Insight, 36, 41
Inspire, 59
Introverts, 158, 160
Iraq, 21, 154, 157, 161

# J

Jack Kornfield
  *The Wise Heart, 127*
James Fowler, 66
James Kouzes, 57
Jeff Weitzen, 73, 98
Jim Collins
  *Good to Great, 78*
Jim Heskett, 57
John Kotter
  *Corporate Culture and
  Performance, 57*

# K

Ken Blanchard
  *The One Minute Manager, 57*

# L

Language, 79
Letting Go, 125, 126, 128
Lucent Technologies, 21, 129
Lynn, Massachusetts, 43

# M

MCI/Worldcom, 97, 105
Mike Armstrong, 97, 108
Mike Willenborg, 63
Millennials, 123, 125, 126
Model, 59
Morristown Rehabilitation
  Hospital, 39

# N

Nicholas Christakis, 66

# O

Opus, 115

# P

Pat Russo, 129, 145
People Value Added (PVA), 72
Peter Sifneos, 78
Plan tactics, 53, 83,
Power Compass, 167, 170
PricewaterhouseCoopers, 110

# Q

Question, 59

# R

R3, 101, 109
RAIN, 127
Richard Gaddy, 62
Robert Greenleaf
  *Servant Leadership, 57*

# S

Sales & Marketing Management
  Magazine, 129, 140
Sam Palmisano, 163
Selling Power Magazine, 130, 140
Serenity Prayer, 126
Sigal Barsade, 65
Speak, 48
Spencer Johnson
  *Who Moved My Cheese, 111*
Spencer Johnson, 57
Sperry Univac, 36
Stories, 79
Strategize, 53, 147
Support, 56, 85
Susan Cain
  *Quiet: The Power of Introverts in
  a World That Can't Stop Talking,
  160*
Sustainable growth, 161

**T**

Talmud, 33
Team Assessment, 116
Think, 48

**U**

Unisys, 62

**V**

Values, 31, 123
Values and Fish Sticks, 31
Viral engagement, 65
Vulnerability, 111

**W**

Warfighters, 145, 148, 152
Write, 48

Rick Miller is an unconventional turnaround specialist, a servant leader, and a go-to Chief. He is also an experienced and trusted confidant, an author, a sought-after speaker, and an expert at driving sustainable growth. For over 30 years, Rick served as a successful business executive in roles including President and/or CEO in a Fortune 10, a Fortune 30, a startup, and a non-profit. In each case, he was recruited from the outside to turn around poor performance in difficult times.

Rick Miller is a Chief not because of his many high-ranking titles, but because of his ability to bring out the best in others—and in himself—using the choices he developed in his Power Compass, a road-tested sustainable growth model he created over the course of his successful career, and which he shares in this book and continues to use with his clients.

Rick has been in demand for the past ten years as a confidential adviser to many of today's most senior executives, and is extensively connected within the global business and leadership communities. Rick continues to serve senior executives by offering broad business experience in six specific areas: customers, competitors, costs, capital, communities, and culture. Rick helps senior leaders ask the right questions.

Rick has earned a BA from Bentley University and an MBA from Columbia University.

For more information on joining the Be Chief team for tips and updates or on working with Rick please visit:

**BEINGCHIEF.com**

CPSIA information can be obtained
at www.ICGtesting.com
Printed in the USA
LVHW05*0430110518
576794LV00002B/20/P